MW00596205

Healthy Eats

101 Biohacking Recipes for Quick, Healthy and Sustainable Weight Loss

Copyright © 2019 *Wendi Francis MS, RD, CPC*
All Rights Reserved

All content is subject to copyright and may not be reproduced in any form without express written consent of the author.

Although the author and publisher have made every effort to ensure that the information in this book was correct at press time, the author and publisher do not assume and hereby disclaim any liability to any party for any loss, damage, or disruption caused by errors or omissions, whether such errors or omissions result from negligence, accident, or any other cause.

This book is not intended as a substitute for the advice of medical professionals. The reader should regularly consult a medical professional in matters relating to his/her health and particularly with respect to any symptoms that may require diagnosis or medical attention.

Cover Illustration, Book Design and Production by Efluential Publishing, a division of eFluential Marketing, LLC.

www.EfluentialPublishing.com

Introduction

So, you are getting ready to make a change...FANTASTIC! To make change, you need inspiration, not motivation!

Our intention in compiling this fantastic book of healthful recipes is to inspire you to be and become more creative with your healthful eating. It is amazing how quick, easy, and fun healthful eating can be if you have the right inspiration.

All the recipes in this book create a synergistic anti-inflammatory, low-glycemic index lifestyle which will enable your body to look and feel healthier and more youthful.

People always say, "Change is Hard." But in our experiences with thousands of clients, change is easier if you have all the tools, inspiration and the right mindset to put those tools to work. As a Dietitian and food psychologist, Wendi Francis, and Dr. Leighow, as a weight loss expert, have been able to help thousands of. A life that was meant to be lived instead of a life that was dull, dreary, painful or maybe even emotionally dead. That is not life. Life, in a healthful body and mind can be lived, enjoyed and celebrated. That is our intention in putting together these recipes. We want you to have a tool to put in your toolbox to help you live an inspired, celebrated and joyful life.

A life in which you feel connected with yourself and others.

A life in which your body does not hurt, ache or suffer from disease.

A life in which you can feel joy.

A life that you live and feel ALIVE in your body and your minds. Many people continue in their unhealthful eating patterns because of habit or emotion. Breaking those patterns by eating different foods in different ways can be the first step in breaking those old, unneeded patterns. Patterns in your diet, dictate your physical and for many, your emotional health. Patterns have the power to create a new you and destroy the old one. By using these recipes, you enable yourself to change your old patterns, recreating yourself to find a more vibrant, more healthful you. By changing your eating patterns and foods, you will not only improve your body and lose weight, but you will also feel better mentally and emotionally.

Don't be a statistic!

Currently, the CDC reports that 76 million people in the United States are obese. That is more than the population of California, Oregon, Washington State, Arizona, Nevada, Idaho and New Mexico combined.

Being obese is defined by a BMI greater than 25 and increases the risk of diabetes 20 times and the risk of heart disease by 32%.

Furthermore, a review of 15 studies published in the Archives of General Psychiatry found that obese people have a 55% higher risk of developing depression.

The list of these statistics can go on, but it is evident that obesity is on the rise in the United States. Furthermore, we know, scientifically, that obesity contributes to specific disease states like diabetes, heart disease, cancer, and stroke. We can also see the significant effect that being overweight can have on your mental health. In our professional experience, we can absolutely say, is this is all true.

Isn't it time to change?

Right now!

Today!
Get Inspired and Get Started!

We know you can do this. Enjoy the process of making this change and continue to

Uncover Your Best You!

In Thanks

We have been wonderfully blessed by God to be surrounded by good family, a wonderful staff and two amazing children. We want to thank our team which has dedicated timeless hours to help our programs succeed and change the lives of people. We also thank Dr. Charlie & Wendi Francis for their collaboration with us, pursuing in the same mission of helping patients lose weight in a healthy sustainable way. Enjoy these "Healthy Eats."

- Dr. Jamie Leighow & JoAnise Leighow

"I wanted to take this opportunity to thank my amazing husband and children; your tireless and abundant love enables me to do all that I do. A special thank you also, to those that helped significantly with this book, Zoe M. DeGeorge, Kristen Cundiff and Karen Chaleki and to all of those that work with me professionally, propelling my expansive thought patterns. Finally, thanks and gratitude to all the patients that I have been honored to work with for the last 25 years. I do not go a day without noticing how enormously blessed I am in my professional life to be able to help so many miraculous people."

- Wendi Francis

List of Recipes

Side Options

Salads

Indoor Holiday Celebrations

Outdoor Holiday Celebrations

Desserts

Shakes

These shakes are healthful alternatives to a solid meal and can be used in place of a meal, as a snack, or before or after an intense workout. You can also freeze them in a plastic container to take on the go or eat frozen for a delicious dessert alternative.

"A healthy outside starts from the inside."

Robert Urich

Iced Morning Mocha

- ✓ 6 ounces Decaf Organic Coffee
- ✓ ½ scoop unsweetened cocoa powder
- ✓ 1 scoop Pure Vitality Vanilla Protein Powder
- ✓ 1 cup Unsweetened Almond or Coconut Milk
- ✓ 10 drops of liquid French Vanilla
- ✓ Stevia
- ✓ 1 cup of ice

1.Put all ingredients into blender container. Blend on high, until creamy and frothy. Serve immediately.

☑ 3 ounces of protein
☐ 1 Serving of fruit

☐ 2 Servings of Vegetables
☐ 1-2 Servings of Healthy fat

Orange Ginger Apple

- ✓ ½ of a Green Apple
- ✓ ½ of an Orange
- ✓ ½ tablespoon of Shredded Ginger (or to taste)
- ✓ 1 scoop Pure Vitality Protein Powder
- ✓ 10 drops liquid Vanilla Crème Stevia

1.Put all ingredients into blender container. Blend on high, until creamy and frothy. Serve immediately.

☑ 3 ounces of protein   ☐ 2 Servings of Vegetables
☑ 1 Serving of fruit   ☐ 1-2 Servings of Healthy fat

Watermelon Summer Treat

✓ 1 cup of Watermelon
✓ 1 scoop Pure Vitality Vanilla Protein Powder
✓ 10 drops liquid Vanilla Crème Stevia
✓ You can add ½ cup water for extra liquid if desired.

1. Put all ingredients into blender container. Blend on high, until creamy and frothy. Serve immediately.

☑ 3 ounces of protein
☑ 1 Serving of fruit

☐ 2 Servings of Vegetables
☐ 1-2 Servings of Healthy fat

Mean Green Supreme

- ✓ 8 ounces Unsweetened Coconut Milk
- ✓ ½ cup of Kale
- ✓ 1 ½ cups of Cucumber
- ✓ 1 small Green Apple
- ✓ 1 scoop Pure Vitality Vanilla Protein Powder
- ✓ 20 drops liquid Stevia

1. Put all ingredients into blender container. Blend on high, until creamy and frothy. Serve immediately.

☑ 3 ounces of protein
☑ 1 Serving of fruit

☑ 2 Servings of Vegetables
☐ 1-2 Servings of Healthy fat

Totally Sinful Chocolate Shake

✓ 1 scoop Pure Vitality Vanilla Protein Powder
✓ 1 cup (8 ounces) Unsweetened Coconut Milk, Unsweetened Almond Milk or Unsweetened Cashew Milk
✓ 1-2 tablespoons Unsweetened all-natural Cocoa Powder
✓ 1 cup of Ice
✓ Stevia, to taste

1.Put all ingredients into blender container. Blend on high, until creamy and frothy. Serve immediately.

☑ 3 ounces of protein   ☐ 2 Servings of Vegetables
☐ 1 Serving of fruit   ☐ 1-2 Servings of Healthy fat

Chocolate Raspberry Delight

- ✓ 8 ounces Unsweetened Almond Milk
- ✓ 1 Scoop Pure Vitality Protein Powder
- ✓ 1 tablespoon Unsweetened Cocoa Powder
- ✓ 1 cup Fresh or Frozen Raspberries
- ✓ 10 drops liquid Stevia

1. Put all ingredients into blender container. Blend on high, until creamy and frothy. Serve immediately.

☑ 3 ounces of protein   ☐ 2 Servings of Vegetables
☑ 1 Serving of fruit   ☐ 1-2 Servings of Healthy fat

Almond Joy

- ✓ 8 ounces Unsweetened Almond Milk
- ✓ 1 teaspoon Unsalted Almond Butter
- ✓ 1 teaspoon Dried and Unsweetened Shredded Coconut
- ✓ 1 tablespoon Unsweetened Cocoa Powder (Organic)
- ✓ 1 scoop Pure Vitality Vanilla Protein Powder
- ✓ 10 drops liquid Stevia

1.Put all ingredients into blender container. Blend on high, until creamy and frothy. Serve immediately.

☑ 3 ounces of protein   ☐ 2 Servings of Vegetables
☐ 1 Serving of fruit   ☑ 1-2 Servings of Healthy fat

Orange Creamsicle

- ✓ 1 scoop Pure Vitality Vanilla Protein Powder
- ✓ 1 small Orange
- ✓ 8 ounces Unsweetened Coconut Milk
- ✓ 10 drops liquid Vanilla Crème Stevia
- ✓ ½ cup of Ice (Optional)

1.Put all ingredients into blender container. Blend on high, until creamy and frothy. Serve immediately.

☑ 3 ounces of protein   ☐ 2 Servings of Vegetables
☑ 1 Serving of fruit   ☐ 1-2 Servings of Healthy fat

Vanilla Shake

- ✓ 1 scoop Pure Vitality Vanilla Protein Powder
- ✓ 1 cup (8 ounces) Unsweetened Coconut Milk, Unsweetened Almond Milk or Unsweetened Cashew Milk
- ✓ 2 teaspoons Vanilla Extract
- ✓ 1 cup Ice
- ✓ Stevia, to taste
- ✓ *For a delicious holiday treat add 1 teaspoon of cinnamon and 1 teaspoon of nutmeg to this recipe*

1.Put all ingredients into blender container. Blend on high, until creamy and frothy. Serve immediately.

☑ 3 ounces of protein   ☐ 2 Servings of Vegetables
☐ 1 Serving of fruit   ☐ 1-2 Servings of Healthy fat

Very Berry Smoothie

✓ 1 scoop Pure Vitality Vanilla Protein Powder
✓ 1 cup (8 ounces) Unsweetened Coconut Milk, Unsweetened Almond Milk, Unsweetened Cashew Milk
✓ 1 cup Frozen Strawberries, Raspberries, Blueberries and/or Blackberries (NO sugar added, preferably organic)
✓ 1 cup Ice
✓ Stevia, to taste (Optional)

1.Put all ingredients into blender container. Blend on high, until creamy and frothy. Serve immediately.

☑ 3 ounces of protein   ☐ 2 Servings of Vegetables
☑ 1 Serving of fruit   ☐ 1-2 Servings of Healthy fat

Breakfast

Breakfast is an essential part of eating. It really does "break the fast" that you have gone through all night. It enables the body to begin metabolically burning fuel getting your mind and body ready for the day.

"A winning effort begins with preparation."
Joe Gibbs

Easy Complete Breakfast Skillet

- ✓ 2 ounces ground turkey (or Grass-fed beef)
- ✓ 2 cups homemade salsa (see below)
- ✓ 1 Whole egg
- ✓ ½ Grapefruit
- ✓ 1 teaspoon real butter
- ✓ Optional: 1/8 avocado

Homemade Salsa:
- ✓ 1 cup diced tomatoes
- ✓ ¼ cup diced onions
- ✓ Cilantro, to taste
- ✓ 1 Garlic clove minced
- ✓ 1 Tablespoon lime juice
- ✓ 1 Jalapeño pepper minced
- ✓ Himalayan sea salt and pepper, to taste

1. Melt butter in a skillet and add turkey
2. Cook until turkey browns
3. Add in salsa and mix to combine, let cook together for 2-3 minutes
4. Crack in egg and cover skillet for 7 minutes or until the egg white is opaque

☑ 3 ounces of protein   ☑ 2 Servings of Vegetables
☑ 1 Serving of fruit   ☑ 2 Servings of Healthy fat

Veggie Breakfast Bowl

Breakfast Bowl:

- ✓ 1 teaspoon coconut oil
- ✓ 1 cup asparagus cut into bite-size pieces (with ends trimmed and discarded)
- ✓ ½ cup shredded kale leaves
- ✓ 1 batch lemony dressing (see recipe below)
- ✓ ½ cup shredded (uncooked) Brussels sprouts
- ✓ 2 eggs cooked however you'd like (I soft-boil mine)
- ✓ Garnishes: 6 sliced almonds and
- ✓ crushed red pepper

Lemony dressing:
- ✓ 1 teaspoon extra virgin olive oil
- ✓ 2 tablespoons freshly-squeezed lemon
- ✓ 2 teaspoons Dijon mustard (NO sugar added)
- ✓ 1 garlic clove minced
- ✓ Himalayan sea salt and freshly-cracked black pepper

To Make the Breakfast Bowl:

1. Heat oil in a large sauté pan over medium-high heat. Add asparagus and sauté for 4-5 minutes, stirring occasionally, until tender. Remove from heat and set aside.

2. Meanwhile, in a large mixing bowl, combine the kale and lemony dressing. Use your fingers to massage the dressing into the kale for 2-3 minutes, or until the leaves are dark and softened. Add the Brussels sprouts and cooked asparagus and toss until combined.

3. Put the kale salad in a bowl, top with 2 eggs, sliced almonds, crushed red pepper and any other desired garnishes. Serve immediately.

To Make the Lemon Vinaigrette:

1. Whisk all ingredients together in a small mixing bowl until combined.

☑ 3 ounces of protein   ☑ 2 Servings of Vegetables
☐ 1 Serving of fruit   ☑ 1-2 Servings of Healthy fat

Complete Breakfast Salad

✓ ¾ cup butternut squash chunks
✓ ¼ cup chopped red onion
✓ 1 teaspoon coconut oil
✓ ½ teaspoon cinnamon
✓ Sprinkle of Himalayan sea salt
✓ 1 cup spring mix or baby spinach
✓ 1 small Granny Smith apple thinly sliced
✓ 2 eggs cooked any way you like
✓ 1 teaspoon extra virgin olive oil, for dressing
✓ 2 teaspoons apple cider vinegar, for dressing

1. Combine butternut squash, red onion, coconut oil, cinnamon and Himalayan sea salt together on a baking sheet and roast in a 450° Fahrenheit oven for about 30 minutes or until squash is cooked through. Remove and let cool.
2. Fill a salad bowl with spring mix and add toppings: roasted squash, apple slices, and red onion.
3. Place cooked eggs on top of the salad. Drizzle dressing over the salad and enjoy!

☑ 3 ounces of protein
☑ 1 Serving of fruit

☑ 2 Servings of Vegetables
☑ 1-2 Servings of Healthy fat

Seaside Breakfast Salad

✓ 2 ounces of canned tuna (in water)
✓ 1 fresh egg
✓ 1 cup of organic arugula
✓ 1 cup of marinated artichoke hearts chopped
✓ Himalayan sea salt and black pepper, to taste

1. Preheat oven to 375° Fahrenheit
2. Place tuna in a small bowl and use a fork to break apart the meat. Add artichoke hearts and toss to combine.
3. Place tuna and artichoke mixture into a small oven-safe dish. I use a small oven-safe skillet.
4. Break the egg on top of the tuna mixture.
5. Sprinkle with Himalayan sea salt and pepper to taste.
6. Bake for about 10-12 minutes, or until eggs are cooked to preference.
7. Serve over arugula.

☑ 3 ounces of protein
☐ 1 Serving of fruit

☑ 2 Servings of Vegetables
☐ 1-2 Servings of Healthy fat

Baked Egg Cups

- ✓ 12 large eggs
- ✓ ½ teaspoon Himalayan sea salt
- ✓ ½ teaspoon ground pepper
- ✓ 1 teaspoon coconut oil
- ✓ ½ cup orange bell pepper, chopped
- ✓ ½ cup yellow onion, chopped
- ✓ ½ cup broccoli, chopped into small pieces
- ✓ ½ cup mushrooms, sliced
- ✓ 2 tablespoons fresh parsley

1. Preheat oven to 375° Fahrenheit.
2. Spray twelve-cup muffin tin with cooking spray or line with silicone baking cups. I spray the silicone baking cups with spray, just to be safe.
3. Place eggs into a large bowl and whisk to combine. Season with Himalayan sea salt and pepper.
4. Meanwhile, heat a skillet over medium heat with 1 teaspoon coconut oil. Add chopped veggies (bell pepper, onion, broccoli, and mushrooms) and cook for about 5-6 minutes, until they're a little soft and the onions are fragrant.
5. Add sautéed veggies into the bowl with the whisked eggs. Add in parsley and mix well.
6. Pour egg mixture into muffin cups evenly. I used a 1/3 cup measuring cup to pour.
7. Bake for 17-20 minutes, or until the egg cups are no longer jiggly and an inserted toothpick comes out clean. Allow cups to cool and enjoy immediately.
8. Serving Size = 2 muffin cups

☑ 3 ounces of protein
☐ 1 Serving of fruit

☑ 2 Servings of Vegetables
☑ 1-2 Servings of Healthy fat

Simple Hardboiled Egg and Avocado Bowl

- ✓ 2 hardboiled eggs chopped
- ✓ 1/8 large avocado chopped
- ✓ 1 tablespoon red onion finely chopped
- ✓ 1 tablespoon red bell pepper finely chopped
- ✓ Himalayan sea salt and ground pepper, to taste

1. Combine eggs, avocado, onion and bell pepper in a bowl. Sprinkle with Himalayan sea salt and ground pepper. Serve and enjoy.

☑ 3 ounces of protein   ☐ 2 Servings of Vegetables
☐ 1 Serving of fruit   ☑ 1-2 Servings of Healthy fat

Brussel Sprout Hash

✓ 1 cup butternut squash, peeled, seeded and cubed
✓ ½ cup small red onion, finely diced
✓ 1 clove garlic minced
✓ ½ cup Brussels sprouts, stemmed and sliced
✓ 1 teaspoon extra virgin olive oil or coconut oil
✓ Himalayan sea salt and freshly ground pepper, to taste
✓ 2 whole eggs

1. Add the butternut squash, onion, and garlic to a pan and cook for 5-7 minutes, stirring occasionally, until soft.
2. Stir in the Brussels sprouts, along with a teaspoon of extra virgin olive oil.
3. Season generously with Himalayan sea salt and pepper to taste.
4. Sauté for 8-10 minutes until the Brussels sprouts are bright green and fork-tender.
5. Make two small wells in the hash and crack an egg into each. Cover and cook until the eggs are set. Serve immediately.

☑ 3 ounces of protein
☐ 1 Serving of fruit

☑ 2 Servings of Vegetables
☑ 1-2 Servings of Healthy fat

Spicy Southwestern Breakfast Bowl

- ✓ 2/3 cup of butternut squash cubed
- ✓ 1 teaspoon of extra virgin olive oil, for drizzling
- ✓ Himalayan sea salt and pepper, to taste
- ✓ 1 teaspoon chili powder
- ✓ 1/3 cup yellow onion diced
- ✓ ¼ cup green bell pepper, diced
- ✓ ¼ cup red bell pepper, diced
- ✓ 1 small jalapeno seeded and diced
- ✓ ½ cup fresh spinach
- ✓ 2 whole eggs
- ✓ 1/8 of an avocado, pitted and diced (optional)

1.Preheat the oven to 375° Fahrenheit. Place the diced butternut squash on a rimmed baking sheet and drizzle with one teaspoon of extra virgin olive oil. Sprinkle with Himalayan sea salt, pepper, and chili powder. Bake until tender, turning once.

2.Meanwhile, cook the onion, bell peppers, and jalapeno in a skillet and sauté for 5-6 minutes until soft. Lastly, add the spinach and cook until wilted.

3. In a separate skillet, cook the eggs to desired preference, seasoning with Himalayan sea salt and pepper.

4. To assemble, put the butternut squash in a bowl and top with the veggie mixture, followed by the egg, and then avocado, if desired. Enjoy!

☑ 3 ounces of protein
☑ 1 Serving of fruit

☑ 2 Servings of Vegetables
☐ 1-2 Servings of Healthy fat

Breakfast Salad

Dressing:
- ✓ 1 tablespoon fresh dill chopped
- ✓ 2 tablespoons lemon juice
- ✓ 1 tablespoons apple cider vinegar
- ✓ 1 teaspoon extra virgin olive oil

Salad:
- ✓ 1 cup chopped kale, stems removed
- ✓ ½ cup spring mix
- ✓ ¼ cup roasted asparagus
- ✓ ¼ cups roasted butternut squash
- ✓ 2 fried eggs

1. Preheat oven to 425° Fahrenheit. Line a baking sheet with parchment paper.
2. Snap the tough bottoms off the ends of the asparagus. Drizzle 1 teaspoon extra virgin olive oil, Himalayan sea salt, and pepper on the asparagus and butternut squash and roast for approximately 15 minutes.
3. Combine all the dressing ingredients in a jar. Put on a lid and shake vigorously until dressing is combined. Set aside.
4. Combine the kale, spring mix, roasted asparagus and roasted butternut squash in a bowl and toss together. Divide on two different plates and top with fried egg and desired dressing.

☑ 3 ounces of protein ☑ 2 Servings of Vegetables
☐ 1 Serving of fruit ☑ 1-2 Servings of Healthy fat

Butternut Squash Baked Eggs

- ✓ 1 cup cubed butternut squash (1/3-inch cubes)
- ✓ 2 large eggs
- ✓ ¼ cup almond milk
- ✓ 1 garlic clove minced
- ✓ 2 teaspoons extra-virgin olive oil
- ✓ 1 cup leek, white and light green parts only, rinsed well and sliced
- ✓ 2 tablespoons chopped fresh herbs (mix of sage and thyme)
- ✓ ½ teaspoon balsamic vinegar
- ✓ (NO sugar added)
- ✓ Himalayan sea salt and freshly ground black pepper

1. Preheat the oven to 400° Fahrenheit and line a baking sheet with parchment paper. Toss the butternut squash cubes drizzled with 1 teaspoon of extra virgin olive oil and a few pinches of Himalayan sea salt and pepper. Roast until the squash is tender, about 20 minutes.
2. Whisk together eggs, almond milk, and minced garlic and set aside.
3. Heat 1 teaspoon of extra virgin olive oil in a cast-iron skillet over medium heat. Add the leeks and a pinch of Himalayan sea salt and pepper and sauté until soft, about 1 minute. Stir in the herbs and roasted butternut squash and cook for another minute. Add the balsamic vinegar and stir so that nothing is sticking to the bottom of the pan. Add the egg mixture and spread in an even layer. Transfer the skillet to the oven and bake for 20 to 25 minutes, or until the eggs are set and the edges are golden brown.

☑ 3 ounces of protein
☐ 1 Serving of fruit

☑ 2 Servings of Vegetables
☑ 1-2 Servings of Healthy fat

Ground Beef Butternut Squash Breakfast Skillet

- ✓ 2 ounces Grass-fed ground beef
- ✓ teaspoon of coconut oil
- ✓ 1 ¼ cup onion, chopped
- ✓ ¼ cup celery stalks, chopped
- ✓ 2 cloves garlic minced
- ✓ ½ teaspoon Himalayan sea salt
- ✓ ¼ teaspoon ground white pepper
- ✓ 1 teaspoon ground cumin
- ✓ 1 teaspoon garam masala
- ✓ ½ teaspoon ground coriander
- ✓ 1 cup butternut squash cooked
- ✓ ½ cup spinach, chopped
- ✓ 1 whole egg
- ✓ 1/8 avocado peeled and sliced

1. Preheat oven to 375° Fahrenheit
2. Cook the spinach in the microwave for about a minute, until wilted. Allow the cooked spinach to cool until it can be safely handled and press them with your hands to squeeze out as much liquid as you possibly can. Reserve.
3. While the spinach is cooling, scoop the flesh out of the butternut squash and set that aside.
4. Add 1 teaspoon of coconut oil into a skillet and add onion, celery, garlic and Himalayan sea salt and cook until the veggies are fragrant and softened, about 2-3 minutes.
5. Add ground beef, white pepper, cumin, coriander and garam masala and continue cooking until the beef is completely brown.
6. Add squash meat and drained spinach and mix lightly, just to dis- tribute the ingredients somewhat evenly.
7. Create a dimple in the mixture and crack an egg into the dimple. Sprinkle the egg with a little Himalayan sea salt and

pepper.
8. Place in the oven to bake for 12-15 minutes, until the eggs are set.
9. Garnish with the sliced avocado and serve immediately.

☑ 3 ounces of protein
☐ 1 Serving of fruit

☑ 2 Servings of Vegetables
☑ 1-2 Servings of Healthy fat

Man's and Woman's Omelet

- ✓ 2 whole eggs
- ✓ 1 cup fresh spinach
- ✓ ¼ cup cremini mushrooms, sliced
- ✓ ¼ cup green onions, sliced fine
- ✓ 4 shakes black pepper
- ✓ 1 teaspoon garlic powder
- ✓ 2 teaspoons coconut oil
- ✓ ½ cup clean salsa (NO sugar added)

1. Using 1 teaspoon coconut oil, sauté the spinach, mushrooms, and onions. Add about half of the seasonings to the vegetables. When done, transfer the cooked veggie mix to one plate.
2. In the same pan, and using the other teaspoon of coconut oil, scramble the eggs and form into a flat pancake of cooked eggs.
3. Transfer the veggies back on the eggs and fold the eggs over to create your omelet.
4. Serve with salsa.

☑ 3 ounces of protein   ☑ 2 Servings of Vegetables
☐ 1 Serving of fruit   ☑ 1-2 Servings of Healthy fat

Turkey Greens Frittata

- ✓ 2 ounces shredded turkey
- ✓ 1 ½ cups finely greens (collard, kale or spinach)
- ✓ 4 large garlic cloves finely chopped
- ✓ ¼ cup onion, chopped
- ✓ 1 whole egg
- ✓ ¼ cup large tomato, sliced (for topping)

1. Stir everything (except the tomato) together until well combined.
2. Pour into a small casserole dish (I use a bread loaf pan), top with the tomato slices and bake at 350 until the egg is fully cooked.

☑ 3 ounces of protein
☐ 1 Serving of fruit

☑ 2 Servings of Vegetables
☐ 1-2 Servings of Healthy fat

Veggie Egg Muffins

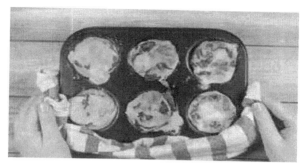

- ✓ 1 teaspoon extra virgin olive oil
- ✓ 1/3 cup yellow onion chopped
- ✓ 1 clove garlic minced
- ✓ 1/3 cup zucchini shredded
- ✓ 1/3 cup red bell pepper chopped
- ✓ 2 whole eggs
- ✓ 1 cup arugula roughly chopped
- ✓ Himalayan sea salt and pepper, to taste

1. Preheat oven to 375° Fahrenheit. Coat a muffin tin with coconut oil spray and set aside.
2. In a large skillet on medium heat, drizzle 1 teaspoon of extra virgin olive oil and sauté onion and garlic for about 4 minutes until tender and fragrant. Add in zucchini and red bell pepper, cooking an additional 2 minutes. Fill each muffin tin about 2/3 full of veggie mixture.
3. In a large bowl, whisk together eggs, arugula, and Himalayan sea salt/pepper and fill each muffin tin evenly, being careful not to overfill.
4. Bake muffins for about 20 minutes, until risen and slightly browned. Enjoy!

☑ 3 ounces of protein
☐ 1 Serving of fruit

☑ 2 Servings of Vegetables
☑ 1-2 Servings of Healthy fat

Spaghetti Eggs

✓ 2 eggs
✓ 1 teaspoon coconut oil
✓ 1 cup spaghetti sauce (NO sugar added)

1. Scramble your eggs as usual.
2. Stir in your leftover spaghetti sauce.
3. Stir until warmed through and enjoy with 1 cup of vegetables and your serving of fruit.

☑ 3 ounces of protein   ☑ 2 Servings of Vegetables
☐ 1 Serving of fruit   ☑ 1-2 Servings of Healthy fat

Southwest Scramble

- ✓ 2 large eggs
- ✓ ¼ teaspoon cumin
- ✓ ½ teaspoon oregano
- ✓ ¼ teaspoon paprika
- ✓ Himalayan sea salt and pepper, to taste
- ✓ 1 teaspoon coconut oil
- ✓ 1/8 avocado
- ✓ ¼ cup zucchini, grated
- ✓ ¼ cup orange bell pepper, chopped
- ✓ ¼ cup red bell pepper, chopped
- ✓ ¼ cup cherry tomatoes
- ✓ 1 cup green onion chopped
- ✓ ¼ cup cilantro, chopped

1.In a medium bowl, whisk together eggs, cumin, oregano, paprika, Himalayan sea salt and pepper until egg mixture is foamy. Set aside.

2.In a large skillet, heat oil on medium-high heat and sauté bell peppers until soft and fragrant, about 4 minutes. Add zucchini, tomatoes and green onions and continue cooking another minute.

3.Add in egg mixture and stir until eggs are cooked, about 3 to 5 minutes. Mix in cilantro.

4.Top and serve with avocado slices, enjoy!

☑ 3 ounces of protein
☐ 1 Serving of fruit

☑ 2 Servings of Vegetables
☑ 1-2 Servings of Healthy fat

Turkey and Butternut Squash Hash

- ✓ 1 cup butternut squash cubed
- ✓ 1 teaspoon coconut oil
- ✓ 1/3 cup yellow onion chopped
- ✓ 1 clove garlic minced
- ✓ 3 ounces 99% fat-free ground turkey
- ✓ 1/3 cup zucchini dice
- ✓ 1/3 cup red bell pepper chopped
- ✓ 1 teaspoon ground cumin
- ✓ 1 teaspoon smoked paprika
- ✓ ½ teaspoon chili powder
- ✓ ½ teaspoon Himalayan sea salt
- ✓ 1 teaspoon fresh parsley finely chopped

1. Bring a large pot of water to a boil and put the cubed butternut squash in the pot. Cook until softened. Drain butternut squash in a colander and set aside.
2. Heat coconut oil in a large nonstick skillet and sauté onion and garlic until fragrant, about 3 minutes. Add ground turkey and cook until crumbled and brown; do not drain any excess liquid.
3. Next add butternut squash, zucchini, bell pepper, cumin, smoked paprika, chili powder and Himalayan sea salt, mixing well, and cook until vegetables are slightly caramelized and crispy, about 5 minutes.
4. Top with fresh parsley, serve and enjoy!

☑ 3 ounces of protein
☐ 1 Serving of fruit

☑ 2 Servings of Vegetables
☑ 1-2 Servings of Healthy fat

Breakfast Taco Bowl

Taco Meat:
- ✓ 2 ounces Grass-fed ground beef
- ✓ 2 tablespoons chili powder
- ✓ 1 teaspoon dried oregano
- ✓ 1 teaspoon ground cumin
- ✓ ½ teaspoon smoked paprika
- ✓ 1 teaspoon black pepper
- ✓ 1 teaspoon Himalayan sea salt
- ✓ ¾ cup water

Salad Ingredients:
- ✓ 1 ½ cups chopped lettuce
- ✓ ½ cup bell pepper, chopped
- ✓ 1/8 avocado smashed
- ✓ 1 whole egg

1. Heat a skillet over medium-high heat. Place the ground beef in the skillet and break up the meat while it is cooking.
2. Drain the grease if necessary and then add all the spices and water. Let the meat simmer for approximately 10 minutes or until much of the liquid is gone.
3. While the meat is simmering, fry the egg and set aside.
4. Grab a bowl and fill with lettuce. Put the rest of the ingredients in the bowl and add the taco meat and fried egg.

☑ 3 ounces of protein

☐ 1 Serving of fruit

☑ 2 Servings of Vegetables

☑ 1-2 Servings of Healthy fat

Cinnamon Chocolate Protein 2 Pancakes

✓ scoops of Pure Vitality Vanilla Protein Powder
✓ 1 scoop Unsweetened Cocoa Powder
✓ 2 eggs
✓ 2 tablespoons Unsweetened Almond Milk
✓ 1 teaspoon baking powder
✓ 1 teaspoon cinnamon
✓ 1 teaspoon coconut oil
✓ 1 cup raspberries or mixed berries

1. Mix the protein powder, cocoa powder, almond milk, cinnamon, baking powder and eggs in a bowl.
2. Put 1 teaspoon coconut oil on a griddle or large pan and slowly add the pancake batter.
3. Cook for about 2 minutes and then flip.
4. Top with raspberries or mixed berries if you choose! You can take one cup of frozen berries and heat briefly on stovetop adding 3 drops of liquid Stevia to make a delicious fruit sauce for the top. See Kaiya's Balsamic Peach Compote under desserts for another delicious topping.

☑ 3 ounces of protein
☑ 1 Serving of fruit

☐ 2 Servings of Vegetables
☑ 1-2 Servings of Healthy fat

Sweet Vanilla Pancakes

- ✓ 2 scoops of Pure Vitality Vanilla Protein Powder
- ✓ 1 teaspoon pure vanilla extract
- ✓ 1 egg
- ✓ 2 tablespoons Unsweetened Almond Milk
- ✓ 1 teaspoon baking powder
- ✓ Cinnamon, to taste
- ✓ 1 teaspoon coconut oil
- ✓ 1 cup raspberries or mixed berries

1. Mix the protein powder, vanilla extract, almond milk, cinnamon, baking powder and egg in a bowl.
2. Put 1 teaspoon coconut oil on a griddle or large pan and slowly add the pancake batter.
3. Cook for about 2 minutes and then flip.
4. Top with raspberries or mixed berries if you choose! You can top with delicious balsamic peach compote from the dessert section of this recipe book.

☑ 3 ounces of protein   ☐ 2 Servings of Vegetables
☑ 1 Serving of fruit   ☑ 1-2 Servings of Healthy fat

Kaiya's Strawberry Peach Fruit-Meal

Crust:
- ✓ 1 cup slivered almonds
- ✓ 1 tbsp. coconut oil
- ✓ 1 tsp. cinnamon

Filling:
- ✓ 2 cups peaches, frozen
- ✓ 2 cups strawberries frozen
- ✓ 2 tsp. vanilla extract
- ✓ 1 tsp. cinnamon
- ✓ 15 drops liquid Stevia

1. Take slivered almonds and put in sealed plastic bag.
2. Crush slivered almonds.
3. Add coconut oil into bag and mix.
4. Place on bottom of pie sheet and sprinkle with cinnamon.
5. In a bowl, put peaches and strawberries with vanilla extract, cinnamon, and Stevia. Combine thoroughly.
6. Take mixture and place on top of almond crust.
7. Cook in oven 375° Fahrenheit for 45 minutes.
8. Makes 4 servings. 1 serving = 1 cup

☐ 3 ounces of protein   ☐ 2 Servings of Vegetables

☑ 1 Serving of fruit   ☑ 1-2 Servings of Healthy fat

Karen and Chris's Scrumptious Strawberry Waffles

1 cup unblanched almond flour/meal (Hodgson Mill)
¼ cup vanilla protein powder
¼ teaspoon baking powder
1/8 teaspoon salt
1/8 teaspoon ground cinnamon
1/8 teaspoon ground nutmeg
1/3 cup unsweetened applesauce
2 eggs, beaten
2 cups strawberries sliced (reserve for garnish)
Coconut oil (liquid or spray) to coat waffle maker

1. Set waffle maker to medium and preheat.
2. In a medium bowl, whisk together almond flour, protein powder, baking powder, salt, cinnamon, and nutmeg.
3. Add applesauce, beaten eggs and water to the dry mixture. Whisk to combine.
4. Lightly coat waffle maker plates with oil using pastry brush or paper towel.
5. Pour waffle batter onto maker plate, close, and wait until waffle maker indicates 'Done'.
6. Remove waffle with fork and repeat steps 4 and 5 until all the batter is used.
7. Garnish waffles with strawberries and serve.
8. Makes 4-8-inch waffles

☑ 3 ounces of protein
☑ 1 Serving of fruit
☐ 2 Servings of Vegetables
☑ 1-2 Servings of Healthy fat

Lunch

Throughout the day your food provides energy and nourishment to your working body.

Feeding it a healthful lunch helps you maintain your energy levels allowing you to complete all the tasks you need with zeal.

"Take care of your body.
It's the only place you have to live."
–Jim Rohn

Easy Salmon Puttanesca

For the Salmon:
- ✓ 3 ounces wild caught salmon
- ✓ ½ teaspoon garlic powder
- ✓ ½ teaspoon Himalayan sea salt
- ✓ ½ teaspoon freshly ground pepper

Puttanesca Sauce:
- ✓ 2 cloves garlic minced
- ✓ ½ cup sun-dried tomatoes
- ✓ ½ cup Roma tomatoes
- ✓ 1 teaspoon extra-virgin olive oil
- ✓ 1/3 cup onion chopped
- ✓ 1 teaspoon fresh lemon juice
- ✓ 1 teaspoon dried parsley
- ✓ 1 teaspoon dried oregano
- ✓ ½ teaspoon basil
- ✓ ½ teaspoon red pepper flakes
- ✓ Optional: 6 kalamata olives, drained and pitted

1. In a food processor or high-speed blender combine all the puttanesca sauce ingredients and pulse for 1-2 minutes. You don't want it fully smooth, so don't over mix.

2. Once done, transfer mixture to a medium saucepan and simmer over low heat for 10 minutes.

3. Preheat oven to 350° Fahrenheit. Line a baking sheet with parchment paper and set aside.

4. Sprinkle salmon with spices.

5. Put salmon in the oven and cook all the way through. The timing will change depending on how thick your salmon is but should take about 5 -10 minutes.

6. Place salmon on a plate, top with puttanesca sauce and garnish. Serve warm with an additional 2/3 cup roasted vegetables of choice to fill your vegetable serving!

7. *If adding the 6 kalamata olives, ONLY use 1 teaspoon of extra virgin olive oil*

☑ 3 ounces of protein

☐ 1 Serving of fruit

☐ 2 Servings of Vegetables

☑ 2 Servings of Healthy fat

Zucchini, Tomato and Basil Steak

- ✓ 2 teaspoons extra virgin olive oil
- ✓ 3 ounces sirloin steak -fat trimmed and cubed (about 1")
- ✓ ½ cup chopped onion
- ✓ ½ bunch chopped scallion
- ✓ 2 cloves crushed garlic
- ✓ 1 cup zucchini cut into 1" cubes
- ✓ ½ cup large tomato
- ✓ Himalayan sea salt and pepper, to taste
- ✓ Handful of fresh basil

1. Heat extra virgin olive oil in saucepan for about 1 minute on medium/low heat.
2. Add steak and stir-fry for about 7 minutes.
3. Add onion, scallion and garlic. Cook for about 2 minutes until onion is translucent.
4. Add zucchini, tomato, Himalayan sea salt and pepper.
5. Lower heat, cover and cook for 20 minutes until zucchini is tender.
6. Stir occasionally and add a little water if the zucchini doesn't lose enough water.
7. Add fresh basil right before serving.

☑ 3 ounces of protein
☐ 1 Serving of fruit

☑ 2 Servings of Vegetables
☑ 2 Servings of Healthy fat

Broccoli Avocado Tuna Bowl

- ✓ 1 teaspoon coconut oil
- ✓ ¼ cup red onion, chopped
- ✓ One 3-ounce can wild caught tuna, drained
- ✓ 1 cup broccoli florets
- ✓ 1/8 avocado
- ✓ 2 teaspoons Bragg's Liquid Aminos
- ✓ 1 tablespoon roasted sunflower seeds
- ✓ ¾ cup cauliflower rice, for serving

1. Heat coconut oil in small skillet over medium heat. Add onion and cook until fragrant, 3-4 minutes.
2. Add broccoli florets and cook until their color has brightened and they're warm throughout. Add tuna, avocado and Bragg's Liquid Aminos to the skillet. Toss to combine and mash the avocado into the mixture a bit.
3. Cook over medium-low heat until everything is warm.
4. Serve immediately, either on its own or over cauliflower rice. Top with sunflower seeds.

☑ 3 ounces of protein   ☑ 2 Servings of Vegetables
☐ 1 Serving of fruit   ☑ 2 Servings of Healthy fat

Curried Avocado Egg Salad

- ✓ 2 hard-boiled eggs chopped
- ✓ 1/8 avocado cubed
- ✓ ½ tablespoon Dijon mustard (NO sugar added)
- ✓ 1-2 teaspoons chopped cucumbers (optional)
- ✓ 1-2 teaspoons green onion chopped
- ✓ 1 teaspoon apple cider vinegar
- ✓ ¾ teaspoon curry powder
- ✓ Himalayan sea salt and ground pepper, to taste

1. Add all ingredients to a bowl and mash together with a fork. Season with additional Himalayan sea salt and pepper if needed.

☑ 3 ounces of protein   ☐ 2 Servings of Vegetables
☐ 1 Serving of fruit   ☑ 1 Servings of Healthy fat

Curry Chicken Salad

- ✓ 2 ounces shredded chicken
- ✓ 6 almonds chopped
- ✓ 3 tablespoons fresh chives chopped
- ✓ 3.5 teaspoons curry powder
- ✓ 1 teaspoon Himalayan sea salt
- ✓ 1 tablespoon Vegenaise
- ✓ 1 cup blueberries

1. Add the shredded chicken, almonds, chives, curry powder and Himalayan sea salt to a large bowl and mix.
2. Add the Vegenaise and mix until combined and then fold in the blueberries.
3. Serve immediately or store in an airtight container in the refrigerator

---

☑ 3 ounces of protein   ☐ 2 Servings of Vegetables
☑ 1 Serving of fruit   ☑ 1-2 Servings of Healthy fat

Orange Marinated Salmon and Vegetable Skewers

- ✓ 3 ounces salmon fillet
- ✓ Juice of 1 orange
- ✓ Himalayan sea salt, to taste
- ✓ 1 teaspoon of extra virgin olive oil
- ✓ 1 garlic clove
- ✓ ¼ cup red bell pepper
- ✓ ½ cup eggplant
- ✓ ½ cup zucchini
- ✓ ¼ cup red onion
- ✓ ½ cup cherry tomatoes
- ✓ 1 peach sliced

1. To make the marinade, cut an orange in half and squeeze its juice into a bowl. You can use a citrus reamer. Add Himalayan sea salt, 1 teaspoon of olive oil and crushed garlic.

2. Remove salmon's skin and bones. With a sharp knife, make a cut between the flesh and skin and cut along the length of the fillet. Remove the skin. The easiest way to remove bones is pulling them out one by one with tweezers.

3. Cut the salmon into bite-sized pieces and transfer them into a bowl with a marinade. Place it in a fridge for at least 15 minutes. If you have the time, let the salmon marinade for a few hours.

4. Meanwhile cut the veggies and peach into the bite-size pieces. Don't cut the cherry tomatoes.

5. If you are using wooden skewers, soak them in water for at least 30 minutes. This will prevent them from burning on the grill.

6. Thread the salmon, veggies and pineapple onto the skewers. Make any pattern you like.

7.Preheat grill on medium to high heat and grease it with olive oil. Grill salmon skewers for about 10 minutes.

☑ 3 ounces of protein

☑ 1 Serving of fruit

☑ 2 Servings of Vegetables

☑ 1-2 Servings of Healthy fat

Chicken Stuffed Squash

- ✓ 3" wide, 3" deep acorn squash, seeded and halved
- ✓ 2 teaspoons of extra virgin olive oil
- ✓ ½ teaspoon Himalayan sea salt

Filling:
- ✓ 3 ounces cooked shredded chicken
- ✓ 1 cup red onion chopped
- ✓ 1 tablespoon fresh rosemary chopped
- ✓ 1 teaspoon dried oregano
- ✓ 1 teaspoon granulated garlic
- ✓ ½ teaspoon Himalayan sea salt
- ✓ ½ cup broth/stock

1. Preheat oven to 400° Fahrenheit and line a baking sheet with parchment paper.
2. Cut the acorn squash in half lengthwise, scoop out the seeds and then brush squash with extra virgin olive oil and sprinkle with Himalayan sea salt.
3. Bake the squash for 25-30 minutes or until squash is tender.
4. Add all the filling ingredients to a large bowl and mix until combined.
5. Scoop about ½ cup of filling into each acorn squash and then bake for another 15-20 minutes or until filling is hot. Serve immediately.

☑ 3 ounces of protein
☐ 1 Serving of fruit

☑ 2 Servings of Vegetables
☑ 2 Servings of Healthy fat

Chicken, Kale and Butternut Squash Soup

- ✓ 1 tablespoon butter
- ✓ 4 cups chopped butternut, peeled and cored
- ✓ 1 bell pepper chopped
- ✓ 1 tablespoon garlic chopped
- ✓ 4 cups chopped kale, ribs removed
- ✓ 2 tablespoons fresh thyme chopped
- ✓ ½ cup fresh basil, chopped
- ✓ 4 cups cooked shredded chicken
- ✓ 6 cups bone broth or stock
- ✓ 1 teaspoon of Himalayan sea salt
- ✓ 1 teaspoon black pepper

1. Heat a large soup pot over medium-high heat and add the extra virgin olive oil. When hot add the butternut and bell pepper and sauté for about 5 minutes.
2. Add the garlic, chopped kale, thyme and basil and thoroughly mix.
3. Add the shredded chicken, broth, Himalayan sea salt and pepper and simmer for 20-25 minutes or until butternut is softened.
4. Serve immediately and enjoy!
5. Makes approximately 4 servings. 1 serving = 1 cup

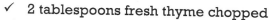

- ☑ 3 ounces of protein
- ☐ 1 Serving of fruit
- ☑ 2 Servings of Vegetables
- ☑ 1 Servings of Healthy fat

Spicy Pepper and Chicken Stir Fry

- ✓ 3 ounces chicken breast cut into 1-inch slices
- ✓ 1 teaspoon coconut oil
- ✓ 1 teaspoon cumin seeds
- ✓ 2 cups of green, red, and orange bell pepper thinly sliced
- ✓ 1 teaspoon garam masala
- ✓ 2 teaspoons freshly ground pepper
- ✓ Himalayan sea salt, to taste
- ✓ Scallions, for garnish (optional)

For the marinade:
- ✓ 1 clove garlic minced
- ✓ 1 teaspoon ginger minced
- ✓ 1 tablespoon freshly ground pepper
- ✓ 2 teaspoons Himalayan sea salt
- ✓ ¼ teaspoon turmeric

1. Place all the marinade ingredients into a zip-top bag. Add the chicken, close the bag, and shake to coat. Marinate in the refrigerator for at least 30 minutes, or up to 6 hours.

2. In a wok or large sauté pan, melt the coconut oil over medium-high heat. Add the cumin seeds and cook for 2-3 minutes. Add the marinated chicken and let cook for 5 minutes. Stir the chicken until it begins to brown, then add the peppers, garam masala, and freshly ground pepper. Sprinkle with Himalayan sea salt. Cook for 4-5 minutes, stirring regularly, or until the bell pepper is cooked to desired doneness. Serve hot.

☑ 3 ounces of protein
☐ 1 Serving of fruit

☑ 2 Servings of Vegetables
☑ 1 Servings of Healthy fat

Baked Mediterranean Chicken

- ✓ 3 ounces chicken breast
- ✓ 2 sprigs fresh rosemary
- ✓ ¼ cup sundried tomatoes
- ✓ 1 ½ cup of cauliflower, cut into florets
- ✓ ¼ cup onion, thinly sliced
- ✓ 1 teaspoon extra virgin olive oil
- ✓ Zest of 1 lemon
- ✓ Juice of 1 lemon
- ✓ 2 cloves garlic minced
- ✓ 1 teaspoon Himalayan sea salt
- ✓ ½ teaspoon pepper
- ✓ 6 pitted black olives sliced

1. In a 9x13-inch baking dish, scatter the fresh rosemary and sun- dried tomatoes evenly on the bottom of the pan. Place the chicken on top.
2. In a medium bowl, stir together the extra virgin olive oil, lemon zest, lemon juice, garlic, Himalayan sea salt and pepper. Pour the mixture over the chicken and place the dish in the refrigerator to marinate for at least two hours or overnight.
3. Preheat the oven to 400° Fahrenheit. Scatter the onion, olives, and cauliflower over the chicken. Bake for 50-55 minutes, or until the chicken is cooked through. Serve warm, topped with additional chopped rosemary if desired.

☑ 3 ounces of protein
☐ 1 Serving of fruit

☑ 2 Servings of Vegetables
☑ 2 Servings of Healthy fat

Bruschetta Chicken

✓ 3 ounces chicken breast
✓ 1 cup small tomatoes chopped
✓ 1 clove garlic minced
✓ 1 cup red onion chopped
✓ 1 teaspoon extra virgin olive oil
✓ 1 teaspoon balsamic vinegar (NO sugar added)
✓ 1/8 teaspoon Himalayan sea salt
✓ Handful basil chopped

1. Preheat oven to 375° Fahrenheit. Sprinkle some Himalayan sea salt and pepper over top, cover and bake for about 35 to 40 minutes depending on the size of your breasts until juices run clear.
2. Meanwhile, combine chopped tomatoes, garlic, onion, extra virgin olive oil, balsamic vinegar, Himalayan sea salt and basil in a bowl. Refrigerate until chicken is ready to be served and spoon over top of the chicken. Enjoy!

☑ 3 ounces of protein
☐ 1 Serving of fruit

☑ 2 Servings of Vegetables
☑ 1 Servings of Healthy fat

Spinach Stuffed Salmon

- ✓ 3 ounces salmon fillet
- ✓ ½ cup green onions, chopped
- ✓ ½ cup mushrooms, chopped
- ✓ 1 cup (packed) spinach, chopped
- ✓ 6 slivered almonds
- ✓ ¼ teaspoon Himalayan sea salt
- ✓ ¼ teaspoon freshly cracked black pepper
- ✓ Few gratings whole nutmeg
- ✓ 1 teaspoon coconut oil

1. Cook the green onions and mushrooms, Himalayan sea salt and pepper with one teaspoon of coconut oil until the onions mush- rooms are soft and golden, about 3-4 minutes.

2. Add slivered almonds and continue cooking until slightly toasted, 1 or 2 minutes, then throw in spinach and cook until wilted, about 30 seconds.

3. Set aside to cool for 5-10 minutes, then stir in nutmeg.

4. Make an incision lengthwise in the salmon fillet, without going all the way through. The skin must remain intact.

5. Sprinkle with Himalayan sea salt and pepper and put the stuffing between the fillet, packing as much as you can down the incisions you just made and mounding the rest on top of the fillets.

6. Delicately add the stuffed salmon fillet to the skillet, skin side down.

7. Cook uncovered for about 1 minute to sear the skin nice and good.

8. Lower heat to low, cover and cook for about 5-8 minutes, depending on thickness and desired level of doneness, until salmon turns opaque.

9. Transfer to oven and set to broil for about 2-3 minutes, until top turns golden and starts to bubble.

☑ 3 ounces of protein
☐ 1 Serving of fruit

☑ 2 Servings of Vegetables
☑ 2 Servings of Healthy Fat

Chicken, Broccoli and Squash Noodles

- ✓ ½ cup broccoli florets
- ✓ 3 ounces chicken breast sliced
- ✓ ½ teaspoon dried oregano
- ✓ 1 ¼ cups zucchini or yellow squash, spiralized
- ✓ ¼ cup cherry tomatoes, diced
- ✓ 1 garlic clove minced
- ✓ ¼ teaspoon red pepper flakes
- ✓ Himalayan sea salt and pepper, to taste
- ✓ 1 tablespoon chopped fresh parsley
- ✓ 1 teaspoon coconut oil
- ✓ 1 lemon, juice of and zest

1. Boil the broccoli florets until tender, then drain and set aside.
2. In a pan sauté the sliced cherry tomatoes, lemon slices/juice and garlic and spices in coconut oil.
3. When tomatoes and garlic begin to cook add in the zucchini/yellow squash noodles and sauté until desired tenderness.
4. Add the zucchini/yellow squash noodles with tomatoes and garlic, broccoli, and cooked chicken breast into a bowl.
5. Garnish dish with the parsley and serve.

☑ 3 ounces of protein
☐ 1 Serving of fruit

☑ 2 Servings of Vegetables
☑ 1-2 Servings of Healthy fat

Salmon Zucchini Bowls

✓ 3 ounces salmon fillet
✓ 1 tablespoon Bragg's Liquid Aminos
✓ 1 small garlic clove crushed
✓ 1 ½ cups zucchini noodles
✓ 1 teaspoon coconut oil
✓ 2 tablespoons water
✓ ½ cup baby spinach
✓ Himalayan sea salt, to taste
✓ Pepper, to taste

1. In a shallow dish, mix Bragg's Liquid Aminos and garlic. Add salmon and turn fillets a few times to coat leaving flesh side down to marinate for 10 minutes or so.
2. Preheat large non-stick skillet over medium heat and spread to coat 1 teaspoon coconut oil. Add salmon in batches (discard marinade) and cook for 4-5 minutes or until golden crispy on each side. Transfer onto platter and set aside.
3. To the same skillet, add water. Cook for a few minutes until cooked but still crispy, stirring once. Add zucchini noodles and spinach. Stir and remove from heat. To serve, place zucchini noodles in a bowl with salmon on top, add Himalayan sea salt and pepper to taste and serve hot.

☑ 3 ounces of protein
☐ 1 Serving of fruit

☑ 2 Servings of Vegetables
☑ 1-2 Servings of Healthy fat

Turkey and Kale Stew

- ✓ 1 large onion finely chopped
- ✓ 5 garlic cloves minced
- ✓ 1 teaspoon extra virgin olive oil
- ✓ 1-pound ground turkey, extra lean
- ✓ 14 ounce can dice tomatoes
- ✓ 1 cup water, boiling
- ✓ 2 teaspoons oregano or thyme, dried
- ✓ ¾ teaspoon Himalayan sea salt
- ✓ ½ teaspoon black pepper, ground
- ✓ 2 bay leaves
- ✓ ½ lemon, juice of
- ✓ ¾ cup kalamata olives, pitted and sliced into halves
- ✓ 4 cups kale, coarsely chopped and packed
- ✓ ½ cup basil, chopped
- ✓ ½ cup parsley, chopped

1. Preheat Dutch oven or large heavy bottom pot over medium heat and add extra virgin olive oil. Add onion and garlic, sauté for 5 minutes or until translucent, stirring occasionally. Add turkey and cook for 12-13 minutes, breaking into pieces and stirring every few minutes.
2. Add diced tomatoes, water, thyme, Himalayan sea salt, pepper, bay leaves, then stir and bring to a boil. Reduce heat to low, cover and simmer for 20 minutes. Turn off the heat and add lemon juice, olives and kale, then stir, cover and let stand a few minutes or until kale is wilted. Add basil and parsley, stir again. It's best to let the flavors "marry" each other for 10 minutes or so. Discard the bay leaves and serve hot.
3. Makes 5 servings. 1 serving = 2 Cups

☑ 3 ounces of protein   ☑ 2 Servings of Vegetables
☐ 1 Serving of fruit   ☑ 2 Servings of Healthy fat

Slow Cooker Blackberry Chicken

✓ 1 medium white onion sliced into rings
✓ 1-pound raw, boneless, skinless chicken breasts
✓ 1 cup fresh blackberries
✓ ½ cup balsamic vinegar
✓ 2 teaspoons garlic powder
✓ 1 teaspoon dried rosemary
✓ Himalayan sea salt and pepper, to taste after cooking

1. Layer the ingredients in your slow cooker in the order listed.
2. Cook on low for 4-6 hours.
3. Serving Size = 3 ounces chicken

☑ 3 ounces of protein
☑ 1 Serving of fruit

☐ 2 Servings of Vegetables
☑ 1-2 Servings of Healthy fat

Lemon Almond Chicken Salad

- ✓ 3 ounces well-shredded homemade chicken
- ✓ ½ cup onion, finely chopped
- ✓ 6 slivered or chopped almonds
- ✓ 1 teaspoon garlic powder
- ✓ 1 teaspoon ground cumin
- ✓ 1 teaspoon coriander
- ✓ Juice of 1 lemon

1.Place all ingredients in a large mixing bowl and stir until well combined.

☑ 3 ounces of protein   ☐ 2 Servings of Vegetables
☐ 1 Serving of fruit   ☑ 2 Servings of Healthy fat

Avocado Salmon Cakes

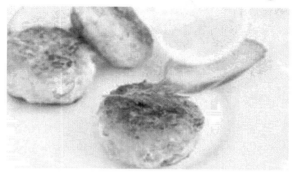

✓ 2 ounces wild caught salmon (canned) 1/8 avocado
✓ 1 egg
✓ 1 teaspoon lemon juiced
✓ ½ teaspoon dried dill
✓ 1 teaspoon coconut oil
✓ Himalayan sea salt and pepper to taste

1. Preheat oven to 350° Fahrenheit.
2. Combine all ingredients in a bowl. Mash the avocado and whisk the egg with a fork. Mash the mixture until it is combined. You don't want to overwork the mixture or make it completely smooth, but you want it well combined and thickened.
3. Heat a non-stick pan over medium-low heat and melt coconut oil. Form the mixture into a patty and place on the pan. Cook for 2-3 minutes per side, turning with a spatula. You want the patties to brown before you turn them. Transfer the patties to a parchment lined baking sheet and bake for 8-10 minutes.
4. You'll know they're done when they have risen slightly in the middle, and they bounce back when pressed with a finger.
5. Serve with 2 cups of fresh greens!

☑ 3 ounces of protein
☐ 1 Serving of fruit

☐ 2 Servings of Vegetables
☑ 1 Servings of Healthy fat

Appetizers

Appetizers can add a sense of elegance to any meal
or as a small plate dinner option for pizzazz.

"Once you start making changes, no
matter how small, suddenly
everything seems possible."

- Oprah Winfrey

Creamy Lemon Basil Spaghetti Squash

Creamy Lemon Basil Sauce:
(Makes 1 Cup but Serving Size = 1 teaspoon)
- ✓ 1 Avocado (½ cup mashed)
- ✓ 6 garlic cloves
- ✓ 1 cup fresh basil leaves
- ✓ 1 tablespoon lemon zest 1/3 cup lemon juice
- ✓ ¼ cup extra virgin olive oil
- ✓ 1/8 teaspoon cayenne pepper (optional)
- ✓ ½ teaspoon black pepper
- ✓ ½ teaspoon Himalayan sea salt

Spaghetti Squash:
- ✓ 1 teaspoon coconut oil
- ✓ 1 cup spaghetti squash cooked
- ✓ ½ cup chopped kale
- ✓ ½ cup cherry tomatoes
- ✓ ½ teaspoon black pepper
- ✓ ½ teaspoon Himalayan sea salt

1. Place all the sauce ingredients in a food processor or blender and puree until smooth.
2. Heat a large skillet over medium-high heat and add the coconut oil. When the oil is hot adding the tomatoes and sauté about two minutes.
3. Add the rest of the ingredients and sauté for another 5 minutes. Add 1 teaspoon of the sauce and mix thoroughly.

☐ Serving of protein
☐ 1 Serving of fruit

☑ 2 Servings of Vegetables
☑ 2 Servings of Healthy fat

Lime Basil Grilled Zucchini

✓ 2 cups zucchini
✓ 2 teaspoons extra virgin olive oil
✓ 1 lime, juice of
✓ ¾ teaspoon Himalayan sea salt
✓ Ground black pepper, to taste
✓ Handful of basil finely chopped

1. Cut each zucchini lengthwise in half and then each half one more time. Drizzle with 1 teaspoon extra virgin olive oil. Set aside on a plate.
2. In a small bowl, add 1 teaspoon extra virgin olive oil, lime juice, Himalayan sea salt, pepper, basil and whisk with a fork.
3. Preheat grill and cook zucchini until cooked but still firm, turning a few times. How long depends on the grill and you know your grill best. Usually it takes a few minutes per side.
4. Cut cooked zucchini into 1" pieces, add to a medium bowl, drizzle with sauce and gently mix. Serve warm or cold.

☐ Serving of protein
☐ 1 Serving of fruit

☑ 2 Servings of Vegetables
☑ 2 Servings of Healthy fat

Stuffed Portobello Mushrooms

- ✓ 2 medium-sized Portobello mushrooms
- ✓ ¼ cup balsamic vinegar (NO sugar added)
- ✓ 2 teaspoons extra-virgin olive oil
- ✓ 3 ounces chicken diced
- ✓ 2 garlic cloves crushed
- ✓ ½ cup onion, finely diced
- ✓ 1 cup fresh spinach Saved mushroom stems
- ✓ ½ cup grape tomatoes
- ✓ ¼ cup fresh basil
- ✓ Himalayan sea salt and freshly ground pepper, to taste

1. Preheat oven to 350° Fahrenheit
2. Wipe clean and remove the stem (save it for later)
3. In a small bowl, whisk together the extra virgin olive oil and balsamic vinegar
4. Pour the mixture into a large zip-top bag and add the 6 mushrooms
5. Seal the bag, allow the marinade to cover the mushrooms, and refrigerate for up to 30 minutes
6. Remove the mushrooms and place them on a baking sheet; bake for 15 minutes
7. While cooking, heat remaining extra virgin olive oil (1 teaspoon) and garlic, add in chopped mushroom stems and onion and let cook for 5 minutes, mixing often
8. Add in chicken, spinach, and roasted tomato; let cook for an additional 5 minutes
9. After the mushrooms have cooked, remove them from the oven (if there is any liquid, gently pour off)
10. Spoon in the filling into each mushroom cap and serve.

☑ Serving of protein
☐ 1 Serving of fruit

☑ 2 Servings of Vegetables
☑ 2 Servings of Healthy fat

Tomato and Eggplant Ragout

- ✓ ½ cup organic diced tomatoes
- ✓ ½ cup eggplant, peeled and cubed
- ✓ 2 garlic cloves crushed
- ✓ 2 teaspoons extra-virgin olive oil
- ✓ ¼ teaspoon red pepper flakes
- ✓ ½ teaspoon garlic powder
- ✓ ½ teaspoon onion powder
- ✓ ½ teaspoon Italian seasoning
- ✓ Himalayan sea salt, to taste
- ✓ Freshly ground pepper, to taste
- ✓ 1 cup fresh spinach
- ✓ 3 ounces of fish or chicken

1. In a large skillet heat extra, virgin olive oil and garlic
2. Peel and cube eggplant and add to skillet
3. Sauté for 7 minutes, mixing often
4. Add diced tomatoes and spices, let cook for 5 minutes (add spinach here), then reduce heat and let simmer for 15 minutes
5. Taste and adjust spices as desired and serve with protein of choice

☑ Serving of protein
☐ 1 Serving of fruit

☑ 2 Servings of Vegetables
☑ 2 Servings of Healthy fat

Balsamic Chicken Zoodle Soup

- ✓ 2 teaspoons extra virgin olive oil
- ✓ 1/3 cup yellow onion chopped
- ✓ 1/3 cup red bell pepper chopped
- ✓ 1/3 cup butternut squash chopped
- ✓ ½ teaspoons granulated garlic
- ✓ 2 teaspoons dried oregano
- ✓ 1.5 teaspoons Himalayan sea salt
- ✓ ¼ cup balsamic vinegar (NO sugar added)
- ✓ 3-4 cups chicken stock/bone broth, low sodium
- ✓ 1 bay leaf
- ✓ 3 ounces cooked shredded chicken
- ✓ 1 cup zucchini, spiralized

1. Heat the oil in a large soup pot or Dutch oven over medium-high heat. Add the onions and sauté for 2 minutes and then add the bell pepper and butternut squash and sauté for another 2 minutes.
2. Add the garlic, oregano, Himalayan sea salt, balsamic vinegar, broth, and bay leaf. Place a lid on the pot and let simmer for 20-25 minutes or until butternut squash are softened.
3. While the soup is simmering spiralize the zucchini into noodles and set aside.
4. Add the chicken and stir to combine.
5. Add the zucchini noodles to the bottom of the bowl and top with the soup. Serve immediately.

☑ 3 ounces of protein
☐ 1 Serving of fruit

☑ 2 Servings of Vegetables
☑ 2 Servings of Healthy fat

Stuffed Mushrooms

- ✓ 2 large white mushrooms
- ✓ ½ cup red bell pepper – chopped fine
- ✓ ½ cup large green bell pepper – chopped fine
- ✓ 2 cloves garlic minced
- ✓ ½ teaspoon onion powder
- ✓ 2 ounces cooked turkey meat
- ✓ Stems from your mushrooms – chopped fine
- ✓ 1 whole egg
- ✓ ¼ cup tomato sauce, NO sugar added

1. Preheat oven to 350° Fahrenheit.
2. Clean mushrooms and gently remove the stems. Set stems aside.
3. Mix all ingredients (except mushroom caps) in a large mixing bowl.
4. Place mushroom caps on a parchment lined cookie sheet.
5. Using a small spoon, gently scoop filling into the mushroom caps.
6. Bake for 20-30 minutes, or until mushrooms have a nice golden-brown appearance.
7. Serve immediately. They are best right out of the oven.

☑ 3 ounces of protein   ☑ 2 Servings of Vegetables
☐ 1 Serving of fruit   ☑ 2 Servings of Healthy fat

Rosemary Roasted Almonds

- ✓ 2 cups skin-on whole raw almonds
- ✓ 2 tablespoons dried rosemary
- ✓ 2 teaspoons Himalayan sea salt
- ✓ ¼ teaspoon freshly ground pepper
- ✓ 1 tablespoon butter

1. Melt the butter in large skillet over medium-low heat.
2. When the butter starts bubbling, throw in the almonds (making sure they're in a single layer) and stir until coated.
3. Add rosemary, Himalayan sea salt, and pepper.
4. Toast the almonds in the skillet, stirring often, until slightly darkened and aromatic (about 8 to 12 minutes).
5. Remove almonds and place on paper towel until cooled to room temperature
6. Serving Size = 6 almonds

☑ 1 ounces of protein
☐ 1 Serving of fruit

☐ 2 Servings of Vegetables
☑ 2 Servings of Healthy fat

Zucchini Chips

- ✓ 4 large zucchinis evenly sliced 1/8 inch thick
- ✓ 2 tablespoons avocado oil
- ✓ Himalayan sea salt
- ✓ ½ teaspoon hot smoked paprika (optional)
- ✓ ½ teaspoon cumin (optional)

1. Slice the zucchini. (Using a mandolin helps keep the slices consistent.) Lay the zucchini slices on paper towels in a single layer. Cover with more paper towels and set a baking sheet on top of the zucchini slices. Press down on the baking sheet, applying slight pressure, squeezing out some of the moisture.
2. Preheat the oven to 235° Fahrenheit.
3. Line several baking sheets with parchment paper. Brush the parchment paper lightly with extra virgin olive oil. Lay the zucchini slices in a single layer on the parchment paper. Fit as many on each baking sheet as possible. Lightly brush the top of the zucchini with extra virgin olive oil. Sprinkle the zucchini slices with Himalayan sea salt. Sprinkle with a little cumin and smoked paprika for extra flavor.
4. Bake for 1 ½–2 hours until crisp and golden. If some zucchini chips are still a little flimsy or damp, remove the crisp chips and place the damp chips back in the oven for a few more minutes. Allow the zucchini chips to cool on paper towels to absorb any extra oil.
5. Serving Size = 1 cup cooked

☐ Serving of protein
☐ 1 Serving of fruit

☑ 2 Servings of Vegetables
☑ 1 Servings of Healthy fat

Butternut Squash Soup with Coconut Milk and Cilantro

- ✓ 2 regular sized butternut squashes - baked and removed from skin
- ✓ 2 cups chicken broth (no sugar added)
- ✓ 1 (14 ounce) can light, unsweetened coconut milk
- ✓ 2 teaspoons dried cilantro
- ✓ 1 teaspoon dried, ground ginger
- ✓ Himalayan sea salt, to taste
- ✓ Fresh cilantro for garnish

1. Place your pre-cooked squash, chicken broth, coconut milk, dried cilantro, and ginger in a large soup pot and blend with a hand blender.
2. Warm the ingredients in the pot on your stovetop.
3. Serve and garnish with fresh, chopped cilantro.
4. Serving Size = 2 cups

☐ Serving of protein
☐ 1 Serving of fruit

☑ 2 Servings of Vegetables
☑ 2 Servings of Healthy fat

Spicy Salmon and Cucumber Bites

- ✓ ¼ cup Vegenaise
- ✓ ¼ teaspoon smoked paprika
- ✓ ¼ teaspoon hot sauce (NO sugar added)
- ✓ ½ pound Cooked Salmon
- ✓ 1 tablespoon minced shallots
- ✓ 1 tablespoon chopped chives
- ✓ Himalayan sea salt, to taste
- ✓ Freshly ground pepper, to taste

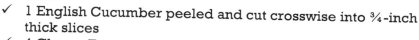

- ✓ 1 English Cucumber peeled and cut crosswise into ¾-inch thick slices
- ✓ 4 Cherry Tomatoes quartered
- ✓ 1 bunch Chive Sprigs (optional garnish)

1. Combine the Vegenaise, smoked paprika, and hot sauce in a small bowl and mix thoroughly. Taste for seasoning and add more hot sauce if you like things spicy.

2. Grab the salmon and flake it into large bite-sized pieces. Place the salmon, diced shallots, chives, Himalayan sea salt, and pepper in a bowl and gently mix in the spicy Vegenaise.

3. Grab the cucumber slices and use a melon baller or teaspoon to scoop out the center of each cucumber slice. Don't dig too deeply or your cups will become open-ended tubes and the salmon filling will fall through when your guests pick them up.

4. Divide the salmon mixture into each cup and top each with a cherry tomato slice and a couple of chive tops.

5. Makes 2 servings

☑ 3 ounces of protein
☐ 1 Serving of fruit

☐ 2 Servings of Vegetables
☑ 2 Servings of Healthy fat

Red Cabbage Steaks

- ✓ 2 cups medium/large red cabbage
- ✓ 1 teaspoon extra virgin olive oil
- ✓ 1 tablespoon garlic chopped
- ✓ 1 teaspoon Himalayan sea salt
- ✓ 1 teaspoon black pepper
- ✓ ½ cup balsamic vinegar (NO sugar added)

1. Preheat oven to 425° Fahrenheit.
2. Slice the cabbage steaks ½ inch thick starting from the top all the way through the bottom (leave the core in).
3. Lay the 'steaks' on a baking sheet and sprinkle with 1 teaspoon extra virgin olive oil, garlic, Himalayan sea salt, and pepper.
4. Bake for 20-25 minutes
5. While the steaks are cooking, heat the balsamic in a saucepan over medium-high heat. Lightly simmer until mixture has reduced by half.
6. Drizzle about ¼ cup of reduction on the steaks before serving.

☐ Serving of protein   ☑ 2 Servings of Vegetables
☐ 1 Serving of fruit   ☑ 2 Servings of Healthy fat

Balsamic Chicken and Strawberry Skewers

- ✓ 3 ounces boneless skinless chicken breast cubed
- ✓ 1 teaspoon Himalayan sea salt
- ✓ 1 teaspoon black pepper
- ✓ 1 teaspoon extra virgin olive oil
- ✓ ¼ cup balsamic vinegar (NO sugar added)
- ✓ 1 cup strawberries

1. Place the cubed chicken in a gallon sized zip-top bag. Toss the Himalayan sea salt, pepper, and extra virgin olive oil into the bag with the chicken.

2. In a separate bowl or cup, add the vinegar. Then pour half of the vinegar into the bag with the chicken. Reserve the rest in the bowl for later.

3. Seal the bag and toss it around in your hands to evenly coat the chicken. Let the chicken marinate in the fridge 2-4 hours. Thirty minutes before you want to make the chicken, soak the wooden skewers in water. This helps to prevent them from burning in the oven.

4. When you're ready to start cooking, place the strawberries in a bowl and pour the reserved vinegar on top.

5. Remove the chicken from the fridge and line a baking sheet with parchment paper.

6. Make the skewers by alternating between cubes of chicken and strawberries. I use 4 pieces of chicken and 3 strawberries per skewer.

7. Place each skewer on the baking sheet and repeat until all the chicken is used.

8. Place a small pan on the stove over medium-low heat. Add any remaining marinade from the bowl that held the strawberries plus the marinade from the chicken into the pot. Let the marinade reduce by at least half while the chicken cooks, whisking occasionally. Adjust the heat as needed to keep the reduction at a steady simmer.

9. Turn the broiler on to high and place the baking sheet on the top rack of your oven, a few inches below the flame.
10. Broil the chicken, turning occasionally, until the chicken is no longer pink.

☑ 3 ounces of protein   ☐ 2 Servings of Vegetables
☑ 1 Serving of fruit   ☐ 1-2 Servings of Healthy fat

Entrees

Nourishing meals sustain our body and our life giving us the energy we need to not just survive in our lives but to thrive in our lives.

"Let food be thy medicine and medicine be thy food."
- Hippocrates

Sheet Pan Chicken Dinner

- ✓ ½ cup zucchini, sliced
- ✓ 1/3 cup asparagus sliced into bite-sized pieces
- ✓ ½ cup butternut squash, chopped into bite-sized pieces
- ✓ 1/3 cup Brussel sprouts sliced in half or quartered
- ✓ 1/3 cup red onion sliced thinly
- ✓ 4 garlic cloves crushed
- ✓ 3 ounces chicken breast
- ✓ 2 teaspoons extra-virgin olive oil

Spice Mix:
- ✓ 1 teaspoon cumin
- ✓ 1 teaspoon onion granules
- ✓ 1 teaspoon fresh thyme
- ✓ Pinch cayenne pepper
- ✓ 1 teaspoon Himalayan sea salt (more to taste)
- ✓ 1 teaspoon pepper (more to taste)
- ✓ 1 teaspoon garlic granule
- ✓ 1 ½ teaspoon paprika
- ✓ ¼ teaspoon ground ginger
- ✓ 4 thyme sprigs

1. Preheat oven to 400° Fahrenheit.
2. In a bowl combine all chopped veggies and garlic.
3. Add in whole chicken breast or halved chicken breast.
4. Pour extra virgin olive oil and spices over veggie and chicken mixture and coat evenly.
5. Add thyme sprigs to the mixture.
6. Place on a lined baking sheet and bake for 25-30 minutes until chicken is fully cooked through. If chicken is done before vegetables, remove chicken and let veggies continue to cook.
7. Add additional Himalayan sea salt and pepper as desired.

- ☑ 3 ounces of protein
- ☐ 1 Serving of fruit
- ☑ 2 Servings of Vegetables
- ☑ 2 Servings of Healthy fat

Italian Style Spaghetti Squash Bake

- ✓ 1 Spaghetti Squash
- ✓ 9 ounces organic boneless chicken breasts baked and shredded
- ✓ 3 cups fresh spinach
- ✓ 1 teaspoon extra-virgin olive oil
- ✓ 1 teaspoon coconut oil
- ✓ 1 clove garlic crushed
- ✓ 1 cup tomato sauce of choice (homemade or jar, NO sugar added)
- ✓ 1 egg
- ✓ 1½ tablespoons Italian seasoning
- ✓ ½ teaspoon red pepper flakes, more to taste
- ✓ 1 tablespoon garlic powder
- ✓ ½ teaspoon freshly ground pepper
- ✓ ¼ teaspoon Himalayan sea salt

1. Preheat the oven to 375° Fahrenheit.
2. Roast spaghetti squash. Cut spaghetti squash in half and scrape out seeds.
3. Line baking pan with tin foil and drizzle with extra virgin olive oil.
4. Lay spaghetti squash halves face down or and bake for about 30 minutes until you can pierce with a fork.
5. Take out roasted squash and scrape out noodle strands using a fork into a bowl, set aside. (leave the oven on.)
6. In a pan over medium heat, heat coconut oil and sauté garlic. Add spinach and sauté.
7. Shred pre-baked chicken. In a large bowl combine spaghetti squash, chicken, and spinach with tomato sauce, egg, and seasonings.
8. Transfer entire mixture into a Pyrex glass baking dish.
9. Sprinkle with red pepper flakes.

10. Bake on 375° Fahrenheit for 10 minutes then broil on high for 5 minutes or until top is crispy.
11. Makes 3 servings

☑ 3 ounces of protein   ☑ 2 Servings of Vegetables
☐ 1 Serving of fruit   ☑ 2 Servings of Healthy fat

Chicken Fajita Roll-Ups

For the Marinade:
- ✓ 2 tablespoons extra virgin olive oil
- ✓ Juice of half a lime
- ✓ 1 clove garlic minced
- ✓ 1 teaspoon chili powder
- ✓ ½ teaspoon cumin
- ✓ ½ teaspoon dried oregano
- ✓ ½ teaspoon Himalayan sea salt
- ✓ Pinch of cayenne pepper (optional)
- ✓ 2 tablespoons cilantro chopped

For the chicken:
- ✓ 3 chicken breasts or 6 thin, 3-ounce, sliced chicken cutlets ¼-inch thick
- ✓ ½ red bell pepper, sliced
- ✓ ½ yellow bell pepper, sliced
- ✓ ½ green bell pepper, sliced

1. In a small bowl, whisk together extra virgin olive oil, lime juice, garlic, chili powder, cumin, oregano, Himalayan sea salt, cayenne (if using) and cilantro. Set aside.

2. Slice chicken breasts lengthwise into 2 even slices and firmly pound the chicken using the smooth side of a meat tenderizer to an even thickness of about ¼ inch.

3. Place chicken cutlets into a large resealable freezer bag and pour in marinade, making sure they are completely coated. Allow chicken to marinate for a minimum of one hour to overnight.

4. When chicken has marinated, evenly place six bell pepper slices in the middle of the chicken cutlet, roll up and secure with a toothpick. Repeat this step until all the cutlets have been rolled up. Place seam side down in a prepared baking dish.

5. Brush tops of chicken with remaining marinade and bake, uncovered, at 375° Fahrenheit for about 25 to 30 minutes or until the juices run clear. Serve and enjoy!

6. Makes 6 servings

☑ 3 ounces of protein
☐ 1 Serving of fruit
☑ 1 Servings of Vegetables
☑ 2 Servings of Healthy fat

Balsamic and Herb Chicken

- ✓ 2 tablespoons balsamic vinegar
- ✓ 2 teaspoons Dijon mustard
- ✓ 1 clove garlic minced
- ✓ ½ teaspoon fresh thyme
- ✓ 1/8 teaspoon cayenne
- ✓ Himalayan sea salt and black pepper, to taste
- ✓ 3 ounces boneless, skinless chicken breasts
- ✓ 1 teaspoon extra virgin olive oil or coconut oil

1. In small bowl, whisk together balsamic vinegar, mustard, garlic, thyme, cayenne and Himalayan sea salt and pepper. Pour sauce into a large plastic baggy and add the chicken breast. Marinate the chicken for at least 30 minutes or even overnight.

2. Heat extra virgin olive oil or coconut oil in a large skillet over medium-high heat until oil shimmers, about 3 to 4 minutes. Using tongs, remove chicken breast from baggy (leaving the marinade inside) and arrange in the pan. Allow chicken to cook for about 7 to 8 minutes, without moving, so a nice golden-brown crust form. Flip chicken over and cook the other side for another 7 to 8 minutes. You'll know the chicken is done when the juices run clear and the inside temp has reached 160-165° Fahrenheit.

3. Remove chicken and place on a cutting board to rest then pour the remaining marinade into the heated skillet. Scrape up any brown bits and allow marinade to bubble up and cook, stirring occasionally.

4. Add chicken back into the skillet, coating well. Serve and enjoy!

☑ 3 ounces of protein

☐ 1 Serving of fruit

☐ 2 Servings of Vegetables

☑ 1 Servings of Healthy fat

Pan Roasted Blood Orange Chicken

- ✓ 3 ounces chicken breast (boneless and skinless)
- ✓ 1 tablespoon garlic powder
- ✓ 1 tablespoon chili powder
- ✓ 1 tablespoon dried oregano
- ✓ 1 tablespoon cumin
- ✓ 2 teaspoons black pepper
- ✓ 2 teaspoons Himalayan sea salt
- ✓ Zest of 1 blood orange
- ✓ 1 teaspoon extra virgin olive oil
- ✓ A few blood orange slices

1. Preheat oven to 425° Fahrenheit.
2. Mix all the spices together with the extra virgin olive oil and thoroughly coat the chicken.
3. Place the chicken in a cast iron or Dutch oven pan and place the orange slices on top.
4. Roast for 30 minutes or until chicken temperature reaches 165° Fahrenheit.

☑ 3 ounces of protein
☐ 1 Serving of fruit

☐ 2 Servings of Vegetables
☑ 1 Servings of Healthy fat

Charmoula Cod

- ✓ 1 teaspoon avocado oil
- ✓ 2 tablespoons lemon juice
- ✓ ½ tablespoon paprika
- ✓ ½ tablespoon ground cumin
- ✓ ½ tablespoon garlic powder
- ✓ 1 tablespoon dried parsley
- ✓ 1 tablespoon dried cilantro
- ✓ 3 ounces raw cod

1. Mix all the ingredients (except the cod) in a small mixing bowl.
2. Lay out your raw cod in an oiled baking dish and spread the sauce over the top of the fish evenly.
3. Bake at 350° Fahrenheit until fish is cooked to your preference.

☑ 3 ounces of protein   ☐ 2 Servings of Vegetables
☐ 1 Serving of fruit   ☐ 1-2 Servings of Healthy fat

Chicken or Beef Apple Stuffed Acorn Squash

- ✓ 1 3" x 3" acorn squash
- ✓ 1 teaspoon real butter or coconut oil
- ✓ 3 ounces ground beef or chicken
- ✓ 2 cups baby bella mushrooms (sliced)
- ✓ 1 small green apple (peeled and diced)
- ✓ 6 silvered almonds

Spice Mix:

2 teaspoons Himalayan sea salt
¼ teaspoon garlic powder
½ teaspoon dried sage

- ✓ ½ teaspoon black pepper
- ✓ ½ teaspoon dried thyme
- ✓ 1/8 teaspoon nutmeg

1. Preheat oven to 375° Fahrenheit
2. Cut the squash in half, scoop out the seeds and place, open side down, on a parchment-lined baking sheet. Bake for 35-40 minutes, or until cooked through. The entire squash will be easily pierced by a fork when done.
3. When the squash has 10 minutes left to cook, heat a pan over medium heat. Melt the butter or coconut oil and sauté the sliced mushrooms for 1-2 minutes. When the mushrooms begin to soften, add the ground beef/chicken to the pan, and season with the spice mix.
4. Break up the meat and cook, stirring occasionally (3-5 minutes).
5. When the meat is almost cooked, add the diced apples. Cook an additional 2 minutes, or until the meat is fully cooked. The apples should still be crisp.
6. Remove the squash from the oven and fill the cavity of each squash half with the meat mixture.
7. Garnish with fresh thyme and slivered almonds (optional).

☑ 3 ounces of protein
☑ 1 Serving of fruit

☑ 2 Servings of Vegetables
☑ 2 Servings of Healthy fat

Stuffed Peppers

Peppers:
- ✓ 6-8 Bell peppers
- ✓ 2 teaspoons coconut oil
- ✓ 1 stalk celery (diced)
- ✓ 3 cups riced cauliflower (rice by placing the florets in a food processor)
- ✓ 4 ounces mushrooms (sliced)
- ✓ 1-2 cloves garlic (minced)
- ✓ 1-pound ground beef
- ✓ 1 tablespoon Italian seasoning
- ✓ 1 handful of fresh sage, basil or thyme
- ✓ Himalayan sea salt and pepper, to taste

Marinara Sauce:
- ✓ 2 (14 oz) cans of diced tomatoes (NO sugar added)
- ✓ 1 (6 oz) can of tomato paste (NO sugar added)
- ✓ 2 teaspoons dried basil
- ✓ 1 teaspoon oregano
- ✓ Himalayan sea salt and pepper to taste

1. Cut the tops off each pepper and remove the seeds and ribs. Preheat oven to 375° Fahrenheit. Fill a large soup pot partially with water and bring to a boil. Parboil the peppers in the water for about 2-3 minutes to soften. Remove the peppers from the water and set aside in a glass baking dish. Fill the bottom of the baking dish with water (about ½ cup). This step helps keep the peppers from drying out.

2. While the water boils, heat a pan over medium heat and add the coconut oil. Stir in the riced cauliflower, celery, garlic, and mushrooms. Cook about 5 minutes, uncovered. Remove the vegetables from the pan and set aside.

3. Add the meat to the pan and lightly brown. The peppers will cook in the oven as well, so don't overcook the meat in the pan. Add the vegetables back to the pan, as well as all the seasonings, and stir.

4. Stuff the filling evenly into the peppers, replace the tops back on the peppers and bake for 30-35 minutes. One stuffed pepper should have 3 ounces of meat to fit the serving size on plan. While the peppers bake, stir together all the marinara ingredients in a saucepan over medium heat. Bring to a light boil then reduce to

simmer for 15-20 minutes. Serve the peppers with marinara sauce and enjoy!

5.Makes five servings. 1 serving = 1 pepper with 3 ounces of ground beef and 1 cup of cauliflower rice and vegetable mixture

---

☑ 3 ounces of protein

☐ 1 Serving of fruit

☑ 2 Servings of Vegetables

☑ 1 Servings of Healthy fat

Creamy Butternut Squash Soup

- ✓ 1 head cauliflower (chopped)
- ✓ 1 small butternut squash (or ½ medium sized squash), diced
- ✓ 2 cloves garlic (minced)
- ✓ 1 stalk celery (chopped)
- ✓ 4 cups Chicken Broth
- ✓ 4-6 fresh sage leaves chopped
- ✓ 1 teaspoon coconut oil
- ✓ Himalayan sea salt and pepper, to taste
- ✓ Sliced scallions, to garnish

1. In a large deep pan or soup pot, add coconut oil along with the chopped cauliflower and diced squash. Cook 2-3 minutes. Add the garlic, celery, and sage and cook until fragrant, stirring often (an- other 2-3 minutes).
2. Pour 4 cups of broth into the pot and bring to a low boil. Reduce to a simmer and cook, covered, until the squash and cauliflower are fork tender (about 10 minutes).
3. Use a slotted spoon to transfer about half the cauliflower florets to a separate bowl.
4. Pour the remaining soup into a blender in 2 batches, and blend until smooth. After each batch, pour the soup back into the pot. Stir in the reserved cauliflower. Season with Himalayan sea salt and pepper, to taste.
5. Serve the soup into bowls garnished with the sliced scallions.
6. Serving Size = 2 cups

☐ Serving of protein   ☑ 2 Servings of Vegetables
☐ 1 Serving of fruit   ☑ 1 Servings of Healthy fat

Lime Chicken Kabobs

✓ 3 cloves garlic minced
✓ 1/3 cup freshly-squeezed lime juice
✓ 2 tablespoons extra virgin olive oil
✓ ½ teaspoon freshly-cracked black pepper, plus extra for sprinkling
✓ ½ teaspoon ground cumin
✓ ½ teaspoon Himalayan sea salt, plus extra for sprinkling
✓ 1-pound boneless, skinless chicken breasts
✓ Wooden or metal skewers
✓ Himalayan sea salt and freshly-cracked black pepper, to taste (optional topping: finely-chopped fresh cilantro leaves)

1. In a large bowl or zip-top bag, mix together garlic, lime juice, extra virgin olive oil, black pepper, cumin and Himalayan sea salt until combined. Add chicken breast pieces and toss until evenly coated. Cover or seal, and refrigerate for 30 minutes, or up to 8 hours.
2. Preheat grill to medium-high heat.
3. Remove chicken from bag and discard the leftover marinade. Thread chicken onto skewers, then season the chicken with a few extra pinches of Himalayan sea salt and pepper. Place skewers on the grill and cook for 6-8 minutes, turning once, until the chicken is cooked through. Remove and serve immediately, garnished with fresh cilantro if desired.
4. Makes 5 servings

☑ 3 ounces of protein
☐ 1 Serving of fruit

☐ 2 Servings of Vegetables
☑ 1 Servings of Healthy fat

Steak Kabobs

Korean Steak kabobs:

1 batch sauce/marinade (see below)
1-pound flank steak or sirloin cut into bite-size pieces
Metal or wooden skewers
2 large red or yellow bell peppers, cored and cut into bite- size pieces
1 red onion peeled and sliced into bite-size pieces
Himalayan sea salt and freshly cracked black pepper

Sauce/Marinade:

¼ cup lemon, juiced and zested
1 tablespoon extra-virgin olive oil
4 cloves garlic peeled and minced (or pressed)
1 tablespoon dried oregano
½ teaspoon Himalayan sea salt
¼ teaspoon freshly ground pepper

To Make the Korean Steak Kabobs:

1. Combine the steak with (half of) the sauce in a large zip-top bag or bowl and toss until the steak is evenly coated. Seal or cover, then refrigerate for at least 30 minutes, or up to 8 hours.
2. When you're ready to cook the skewers, heat grill to medium-high heat.
3. Thread the skewers alternately with the marinated steak, peppers and onions. Brush each skewer liberally with the remaining marinade, and season each with a pinch of Himalayan sea salt and pepper. Grill the skewers for 2-3 minutes per side, turning once, or until the steak is cooked to your desired level of doneness. Remove skewers from grill and let rest for 5 minutes. Brush each kabob evenly with the remaining sauce (the half that was not used for the marinade). Serve immediately.

To Make the Sauce:

1. Whisk all ingredients together until combined. Set aside half of the sauce for a dipping sauce, and half for a marinade.
2. Makes 5 servings.

☑ 3 ounces of protein
☐ 1 Serving of fruit

☑ 2 Servings of Vegetables
☑ 1 Servings of Healthy fat

Zoodles Marinara

- ✓ 1 tablespoon extra-virgin olive oil
- ✓ ½ cup diced white onions
- ✓ 6 garlic cloves peeled and minced (or pressed)
- ✓ 1 (28-ounce) can diced tomatoes (NO sugar added)
- ✓ ½ cup roughly chopped fresh basil leaves, loosely packed
- ✓ 1½ teaspoons Himalayan sea salt
- ✓ ¼ teaspoon black pepper
- ✓ 1/8 teaspoon crushed red pepper flakes (or a pinch of cayenne)
- ✓ 2 large zucchinis, spiralized

1. Heat extra virgin olive oil in a large sauté pan over medium-high heat. Add onions and sauté for 5 minutes, stirring occasionally, until the onions are soft and translucent.

2. Add garlic and sauté for 1 minute, stirring frequently, until fragrant. Add the tomatoes, tomato paste, basil, Himalayan sea salt, pepper, and crushed red pepper flakes, then stir to combine.

3. Continue cooking until the sauce reaches a simmer. Then reduce heat to medium-low and continue to let the sauce simmer for about 15 minutes, or until the oil on the surface is a deep orange and the sauce is reduced and thickened. Taste, and season the sauce with additional Himalayan sea salt and pepper if needed.

4. Add in the spiralized zucchini and toss until evenly coated with sauce. Continue to cook for 2-3 minutes until the noodles are slightly softened. Remove from the heat and serve immediately.

5. Serving Size = 2 Cups

- ☐ Serving of protein
- ☐ 1 Serving of fruit
- ☑ 2 Servings of Vegetables
- ☑ 1-2 Servings of Healthy fat

Coconut Crusted Cod

- ✓ 1-pound wild caught cod
- ✓ ¼ cup coconut milk
- ✓ 6 tablespoons shredded coconut
- ✓ 1 teaspoon paprika
- ✓ 1 teaspoon garlic powder
- ✓ 2 cups of asparagus
- ✓ 1 tablespoon coconut oil
- ✓ Himalayan sea salt and pepper to taste

1. Preheat the oven to 400° Fahrenheit.
2. Wash and trim the asparagus, cover with 1 tablespoon of melted coconut oil and place in the oven.
3. Place the coconut milk in a shallow bowl.
4. In a separate shallow bowl, combine the Himalayan sea salt, pepper, paprika and garlic powder.
5. Place the cod in the milk for 1 minute on each side. Dip in the shredded coconut mixture, coating both sides. Place the "breaded" cod on a parchment-lined baking sheet and bake for 12-15 minutes, until cooked through and flaky.
6. Remove both the asparagus and the cod from the oven and serve.
7. Makes 5 servings. 1 serving = 3 ounces of cod with the 2 cups of asparagus

---

☑ 3 ounces of protein
☐ 1 Serving of fruit

☑ 2 Servings of Vegetables
☑ 2 Servings of Healthy fat

Butternut Squash Noodle Hash

- ✓ 1 teaspoon real butter
- ✓ 1 ½ cups butternut squash, spiraled
- ✓ ½ cup chopped kale
- ✓ ¼ teaspoon ground ginger
- ✓ ½ teaspoon onion powder
- ✓ 1/8-¼ teaspoon crushed red pepper
- ✓ Himalayan sea salt and pepper
- ✓ 1 tablespoon Braggs liquid aminos
- ✓ 2 eggs
- ✓ Optional garnish: fresh dill

1. Heat your oven to 400° Fahrenheit and heat a cast iron pan over medium heat.
2. Melt the butter in the pan and add the squash noodles and kale.
3. Season the vegetables with the ginger, onion, red pepper. Sprinkle in a dash of Himalayan sea salt and pepper and stir.
4. Cook for about 5 minutes, stirring occasionally.
5. Toss in the Braggs liquid aminos, cover with a lid and cook for an additional 1-2 minutes, until the noodles are softened.
6. Flatten the noodles into the pan with the back of a spatula and make 2 wells with a spoon. Crack the eggs into the wells and transfer the pan to the oven.
7. Bake for 6-8 minutes, until the egg whites are set.
8. Optional: garnish with fresh dill.

☑ 3 ounces of protein
☐ 1 Serving of fruit

☑ 2 Servings of Vegetables
☑ 1 Servings of Healthy fat

Garlic Lover's Salmon

- ✓ 3 ounces salmon
- ✓ 1 teaspoon butter
- ✓ 2 cloves garlic peeled and roughly chopped
- ✓ 2 tablespoons freshly-squeezed lemon juice, plus extra lemon wedges for serving
- ✓ Himalayan sea salt and pepper
- ✓ ¼ cup chopped fresh Italian parsley
- ✓ ¼ cup thinly sliced green onions

1. Heat oven to 375° Fahrenheit. Or heat a grill to medium heat. Line a large baking dish with a large piece of aluminum foil.
2. In a small saucepan, heat butter over medium-high heat until melt- ed. Stir in the garlic and cook for 1-2 minutes until fragrant. (You want the garlic to be partly- but not fully-cooked.) Remove from heat and stir in the lemon juice.
3. Using a pastry brush, brush a tablespoon of the butter mixture on the foil until it is evenly covered. Lay the salmon out on the foil. Pour the remainder of the butter-garlic mixture on top of the salmon and brush it until it evenly covers the salmon. Season the salmon with a few generous pinches of Himalayan sea salt and pepper.
4. Fold the sides of the aluminum foil up and over the top of the salmon until it is completely enclosed. (If your sheet of foil is not large enough, just place a second sheet of foil on top and fold the edges so that it forms a sealed packet.)

5.To Cook in The Oven: Bake for 10-15 minutes, or until the salmon is almost completely cooked through. (Cooking times will vary on the thickness of your salmon, so I recommend checking it a few minutes early if you have a thinner cut of salmon.) Remove the salmon from the oven and carefully open and pull back the aluminum foil so that the top of the fish is completely exposed. Change the oven setting to broil, then return the fish to the oven and broil for 3-4 minutes, or until the top of the salmon and the garlic are slightly golden and the fish is cooked through. (Keep a close eye on the salmon while broiling to be sure that the garlic does not burn.)

6. To Cook on The Grill: Carefully transfer the packet of salmon to the grill, and grill for 12-14 minutes, or until the salmon is almost completely cooked through. (Cooking times will vary on the thickness of your salmon, so I recommend checking it a few minutes early if you have a thinner cut of salmon.) Carefully open and pull back the aluminum foil so that the top of the fish is completely exposed. Continue cooking for 3-4 minutes, or until the top of the salmon and the garlic are slightly golden and the fish is cooked through.

7.Remove salmon from the oven or grill. Sprinkle the top of the salmon evenly with parsley and green onions and serve immediately.

☑ 3 ounces of protein   ☑ 2 Servings of Vegetables
☐ 1 Serving of fruit   ☑ 2 Servings of Healthy fat

Side Options

Side options to our meal can either complement or detract. These healthful and delicious side options are sure to add a complementary flavor to anything you serve.

"One cannot think well, love well, sleep well, if one has not dined well."
-Virginia Woolf

"Pasta" Salad

For the noodles:
- ✓ 1 large broccoli stem spiraled
- ✓ 1 large zucchini spiraled
- ✓ 2 yellow squash spiraled
- ✓ 1 red onion spiraled

Everything else:
- ✓ ½ cup roasted red peppers
- ✓ ¼ cup roasted garlic
- ✓ ½ cup broccoli florets, finely chopped

Dressing:
- ✓ 2 tablespoons extra-virgin olive oil
- ✓ 1 tablespoon Italian seasoning
- ✓ 1 ½ tablespoons apple cider vinegar
- ✓ ½ lemon, juiced
- ✓ ½ teaspoon Himalayan pink sea salt
- ✓ ½ teaspoon freshly ground pepper
- ✓ Optional: ¼–½ teaspoon red pepper flakes

1. Spiralize veggies and set aside. Chop additional veggies and place in the bowl.
2. In a separate bowl, whisk together dressing ingredients. Pour over salad. Taste and adjust spices as desired. Serve immediately.
3. Serving Size = 2 cups of vegetables and 1-2 teaspoons of the dressing

---

☐ Serving of protein
☐ 1 Serving of fruit

☑ 2 Servings of Vegetables
☑ 1-2 Servings of Healthy fat

Spanish Cauliflower Rice

- ✓ 1-2 teaspoons coconut oil
- ✓ 2 cups riced cauliflower
- ✓ 1 teaspoon crushed tomatoes
- ✓ 2 teaspoons garlic powder
- ✓ 2 teaspoons onion powder
- ✓ 2 teaspoons ground cumin
- ✓ 1 teaspoon chili powder
- ✓ Himalayan sea salt, to taste

1. In a skillet, warm the coconut oil and then add the cauliflower.
2. Cook until it has almost reached the level of tenderness you prefer.
3. Stir in the crushed tomatoes and spices and stir well to combine.
4. Season with Himalayan sea salt to taste and serve.

☐ Serving of protein
☐ 1 Serving of fruit

☑ 2 Servings of Vegetables
☑ 1-2 Servings of Healthy fat

Easy Roasted Eggplant

- ✓ 2 medium eggplants
- ✓ 12 cloves peeled garlic
- ✓ 1 tablespoon extra-virgin olive oil
- ✓ ¼ cup chopped onion
- ✓ ¼ cup chopped scallion (green part)
- ✓ Himalayan sea salt and pepper, to taste
- ✓ For a kick, add freshly chopped hot pepper

1. Make six 1" slits around each eggplant
2. Stuff garlic in each slit and coat with extra-virgin olive oil
3. Wrap with heavy foil paper
4. Add directly to burner and roast on low/medium heat for about 10 minutes on each side (until eggplant is soft)
5. Let rest for 5 minutes
6. Open foil and cut straight down the middle and scoop out inside and transfer to a bowl
7. Mix thoroughly to ensure garlic is mashed. Add onion, scallion, Himalayan sea salt and pepper. Enjoy!
8. Serving Size = 2 cups

☐ Serving of protein
☐ 1 Serving of fruit

☑ 2 Servings of Vegetables
☑ 1-2 Servings of Healthy fat

Sautéed Mushroom Blueberry Chard

- ✓ 2 teaspoons extra-virgin olive oil
- ✓ 5 cloves finely chopped garlic
- ✓ ¼ cup sliced onion
- ✓ 1 cup sliced portobello mushroom
- ✓ ¾ cup chopped chard
- ✓ Himalayan sea salt to taste
- ✓ 1 cup fresh blueberries and/or raspberries for serving

1. Heat extra-virgin olive oil in pan and add garlic and onion. Sauté for about 2 minutes until onion is translucent.
2. Add sliced mushrooms and cook for 5 minutes.
3. Add chard and cook for 2 minutes, until wilted. Do not overcook.
4. Add Himalayan sea salt to taste.
5. Remove from heat and sprinkle blueberries and/or raspberries right before serving.
6. Enjoy!

☐ Serving of protein
☐ 1 Serving of fruit

☑ 2 Servings of Vegetables
☑ 1-2 Servings of Healthy fat

Baked Candied Butternut Squash

- ✓ ½ large butternut squash, peeled, seeded, and cut into 1-inch cubes
- ✓ 1 tablespoon grapeseed oil
- ✓ 1 tablespoon Stevia
- ✓ ½ teaspoon ground cinnamon
- ✓ ½ teaspoon nutmeg
- ✓ Unsalted butter (for greasing)

1. Mix all ingredients in a bowl with a spoon
2. Lightly coat the bottom of a glass bowl with unsalted butter
3. Place the mixture into the glass bowl
4. Cover with foil and bake at 350° Fahrenheit for 1-2 hours, or until tender
5. Remove foil for last half hour of cooking time
6. Serving Size = 1 cup

☐ Serving of protein
☐ 1 Serving of fruit

☑ 2 Servings of Vegetables
☑ 1-2 Servings of Healthy fat

Grilled Leek and Roasted Bell Pepper Salsa

- ✓ 1 small/medium leek
- ✓ 2 green bell peppers
- ✓ 3-4 large tomatoes chopped (yields about 4 cups)
- ✓ 1 cup chopped cilantro
- ✓ 1 tablespoon minced garlic
- ✓ 1 tablespoon chopped jalapeno (or more if you want it spicy)
- ✓ ¼ cup lime
- ✓ 1 teaspoon extra virgin olive oil
- ✓ ½ teaspoon black pepper, or to taste
- ✓ 1 teaspoon Himalayan sea salt, or to taste

1. Preheat grill to 450° Fahrenheit.
2. Cut the green tops off the leeks and trim off the root on the bottom. Brush the leeks and bell peppers with 1 teaspoon of extra-virgin olive oil.
3. Place leeks on the grill and roast for about 2-3 minutes each side and remove from grill.
4. Add the peppers and roast about 8-10 minutes. Periodically rotate the peppers. You want skins to be charred.
5. Place peppers in a bowl and cover with plastic wrap to let the peppers sweat for about 8 minutes.
6. Combine the tomato, cilantro, garlic, jalapeno, lime, pepper and Himalayan sea salt in a large bowl and mix.
7. Remove the outer layers of the leeks that are too charred. Slide the leek in half and then thinly slice. Add to the salsa.

8. Use a paring knife and carefully scrape the charred skin of the bell peppers. De-seed the pepper, chop and add to salsa.

9. If you prefer less chunky salsa, you can place mixture in the blender or food processor and pulse until you reach desired texture.

10. Makes approximately 6 cups. 1 serving = 2 cups

☐ Serving of protein   ☑ 2 Servings of Vegetables
☐ 1 Serving of fruit   ☑ 1-2 Servings of Healthy fat

Dijon and Apple Brussel Sprouts

- ✓ 1 teaspoon extra virgin olive oil
- ✓ 2 cups Brussel sprouts quartered
- ✓ 2 garlic cloves chopped
- ✓ 1 small green apple peeled and diced
- ✓ ¼ cup Dijon mustard
- ✓ ½ cup bone broth or vegetable stock
- ✓ Zest of 1 lemon
- ✓ 1/8 teaspoon cayenne pepper
- ✓ 1 teaspoon Himalayan sea salt
- ✓ 1 teaspoon black pepper
- ✓ 6 slivered almonds (for garnish)

1. Preheat oven to 425° Fahrenheit and heat a large skillet or cast-iron pan to medium/high heat and add extra virgin olive oil.
2. Cut the Brussel sprouts in quarters or halves if small. Add them to the hot pan and let sear for about five minutes.
3. While the sprouts are cooking, chop of the garlic and apple and then add them to the pan and stir. Cook for another 2-3 minutes.
4. Mix together the Dijon, broth, lemon zest, cayenne, Himalayan sea salt and pepper and add the liquid to the Brussels sprouts.
5. Place in the oven and bake for approximately 15 minutes and then turn the oven to broil and cook for another 3-4 minutes or until slightly crisp on top. Watch carefully so they do not burn.
6. Pull the pan out and top with the slivered almonds and serve while hot

---

☐ Serving of protein
☐ 1 Serving of fruit

☑ 2 Servings of Vegetables
☐ 1-2 Servings of Healthy fat

Zesty Cauliflower Tabbouleh

✓ 1 head cauliflower
✓ 4 tomatoes
✓ 1 cup cilantro chopped
✓ ¼ cup lemon juice
✓ ¼ cup lime juice
✓ 2 teaspoons garlic powder
✓ Himalayan sea salt and black pepper, to taste

1.Grate the entire head of cauli flower (stem and leaves omitted), so that it resembles quinoa or rice. I use a hand grater, although a food processor would be faster. Place into a large mixing bowl.
2. Dice tomatoes and finely chop cilantro.
3. Mix together the tomatoes, cilantro, and grated cauliflower.
4. Add the lemon juice, lime juice, Himalayan sea salt, black pepper, and garlic powder. Mix well.
5. Serve and enjoy!
6. Makes approximately 8 cups. 1 serving = 2 cups.

☐ Serving of protein
☐ 1 Serving of fruit

☑ 2 Servings of Vegetables
☐ 1-2 Servings of Healthy fat

Grilled Veggie Salad Platter

- ✓ 4 medium zucchinis
- ✓ 1 medium yellow squash
- ✓ 1 red bell pepper
- ✓ 1 yellow bell pepper
- ✓ 1 red onion thinly sliced
- ✓ 1 lb. asparagus ends trimmed
- ✓ 1 teaspoon extra-virgin olive oil, for drizzling

For the sauce:
- ✓ ¼ cup Vegenaise
- ✓ Juice of 1 lime
- ✓ 2 cloves garlic crushed
- ✓ 1 teaspoon cumin
- ✓ Himalayan sea salt and pepper, to taste

1. Slice the zucchini and squash in half lengthwise and then into ½-inch thick slices. In a medium bowl, whisk together all the ingredients for the sauce. Season to taste with Himalayan sea salt and pepper. Set aside.
2. Preheat the grill to low heat. Lightly drizzle the vegetables with 1 teaspoon extra virgin olive oil and toss to coat. Working in batches, place the vegetables on the grill in a single layer. Close the lid and cook for 10-12 minutes, turning once. Transfer to a serving plate and serve with the cumin sauce.
3. Serving Size = 2 cups

☐ Serving of protein
☐ 1 Serving of fruit

☑ 2 Servings of Vegetables
☐ 1-2 Servings of Healthy fat

BBQ Zucchini

- ✓ 2 cups zucchini quartered
- ✓ 1 tablespoon garlic powder
- ✓ 1 tablespoon onion powder
- ✓ ¼ teaspoon Himalayan sea salt
- ✓ ½ teaspoon black pepper
- ✓ 2 teaspoons extra virgin olive oil

1. Place all ingredients in a plastic bag, and gently shake until the zucchini is coated in the extra virgin olive oil and spices.
2. Place on BBQ grill and cook.
3. When the zucchini is cooked to your liking, remove from the grill and allow to cool. These retain A LOT of heat. So cooling time is essential.

☐ Serving of protein
☐ 1 Serving of fruit

☑ 2 Servings of Vegetables
☑ 1-2 Servings of Healthy fat

Creamy Cauliflower and Leek Soup

- ✓ 3 tablespoons extra virgin olive oil
- ✓ 2 large leeks (root and tough dark green tops removed, cleaned and medium chopped)
- ✓ 2 stalks celery cleaned and medium chopped
- ✓ 3 cloves garlic finely chopped
- ✓ 1 large head of cauliflower (cleaned, green stem and leaves removed and cut into 2-inch florets)
- ✓ 1-quart vegetable stock
- ✓ 3 cups water
- ✓ 1 bay leaf
- ✓ 1 ½ teaspoons apple cider vinegar
- ✓ About 1 tablespoon Himalayan sea salt, (add more if needed)
- ✓ About 1 teaspoon coarse black pepper, more or less to taste
- ✓ Finely chopped chives for garnish

1. In a large soup pot or Dutch oven, heat the extra virgin olive oil over medium-high heat. Add the leeks, celery, and a big pinch of Himalayan sea salt and sauté until soft, about 5-6 minutes. Add the garlic, stir, and cook another minute until very fragrant, being careful not to burn the garlic.

2. Add the stock, 2 cups water, 2 teaspoons Himalayan sea salt, ½ teaspoon pepper and the bay leaf, then bring to a boil.

3. Add the cauliflower florets and turn the heat to medium. Simmer 30 minutes until the cauliflower is fork tender. Discard the bay leaf. Puree the soup with a hand blender, or in small batches in a high-speed blender or food processor until very smooth.

4. Add the pureed soup back to the pot and stir in vinegar and ½ to 1 cup more stock or water (depending on desired texture). Caution:

Be very careful when pureeing hot liquid in a blender or food processor as hot liquid expands. Never fill the blender or food processor more than ¼ full of a hot mixture. Work in very small batches until all of the soup is pureed.

5. Garnish with fresh chopped chives. Chopped parsley or raw pumpkin seeds are also great additions but make sure to use the correct serving sizes! This soup can be stored in the refrigerator in an airtight glass container for up to 3 days. It also freezes well.

6. Serving Size = 1 Cup

☐ Serving of protein
☐ 1 Serving of fruit

☑ 2 Servings of Vegetables
☑ 1-2 Servings of Healthy fat

Curry Cauliflower

✓ 2 cups cauliflower
✓ 2 teaspoons extra virgin olive oil
✓ Garlic powder, to taste
✓ Onion powder, to taste
✓ Curry powder, to taste

1. Preheat oven to 350° Fahrenheit.
2. Break your cauliflower into bite-sized pieces.
3. Put 1 teaspoon of extra virgin olive oil on the tray.
4. Place the cauliflower on the cookie sheet in a single layer.
5. Pour another teaspoon of the extra virgin olive oil over the cauliflower.
6. Sprinkle generous amounts of all spices over the cauliflower; about 1-2 tablespoons of each.
7. Place cookie sheet in oven and cook until the cauliflower has some golden edges and is easily pierced with a fork.
8. Allow to cool.

☐ Serving of protein
☐ 1 Serving of fruit

☑ 2 Servings of Vegetables
☑ 1-2 Servings of Healthy fat

Balsamic Glazed Meatballs

- ✓ 1-pound ground beef
- ✓ 3 tablespoons water
- ✓ 1 teaspoon garlic powder
- ✓ 1 teaspoon onion powder
- ✓ 1 tablespoon dried parsley
- ✓ Himalayan sea salt and pepper, to taste

For the reduction:
- ✓ 1 cup balsamic vinegar (NO sugar added)
- ✓ 1 tablespoon coconut oil

1. Preheat oven to 375° Fahrenheit.
2. In saucepan, heat the balsamic vinegar over medium heat to bring to a slow boil. (You want small bubbles, but not big bubbles in the center of the vinegar.) Whisk often until the vinegar reduces by half and thickens (about 15 minutes). Stir the coconut oil into the vinegar and remove from the heat.
3. Season the ground beef with the garlic, onion, Himalayan sea salt and pepper. Add 2 teaspoons of parsley, saving the rest to garnish at the end. Using your hands, combine the water with the ground beef and form 16-20 (depending on size) meatballs.
4. Bake the meatballs for 10 minutes. Pour the reduction over the meatballs and return to the oven to finish cooking (about 5-8 minutes).
5. Sprinkle with the leftover teaspoon of parsley and serve the meatballs, saving the excess reduction for dipping.
6. Makes 5 servings. 1 serving = 3 ounce.

☑ 3 ounces of protein   ☐ 2 Servings of Vegetables
☐ 1 Serving of fruit   ☑ 1 Servings of Healthy fat

Caramelized Onion Green Beans with Toasted Almonds

- ✓ 1 ½ cups green beans, stems trimmed
- ✓ ½ cup onion, thinly sliced
- ✓ 1 teaspoon freshly grated garlic
- ✓ 1 teaspoon butter
- ✓ 6 diced almonds
- ✓ Himalayan sea salt and pepper, to taste

1. In a large saucepan, add water and bring to boil. Add green beans and cook for a few minutes until beans are crisp. Remove beans from water and place into an ice bath to stop the cooking process.

2. In a large sauté pan, melt butter over medium heat and add onions and stevia if you wish, stirring frequently, and cook for about 25 minutes, or until caramelized.

3. In a small pan, heat almonds over medium heat until golden brown, about 5 minutes.

4. Add the caramelized onions to the green beans and season with Himalayan sea salt and pepper. Top with toasted almonds.

☐ Serving of protein
☐ 1 Serving of fruit

☑ 2 Servings of Vegetables
☑ 2 Servings of Healthy fat

Herb Baked Butternut Squash

- ✓ 1 butternut squash (2 ½-3 cups)
- ✓ 2 teaspoons extra-virgin olive oil
- ✓ 1 lemon juiced
- ✓ 2 cloves minced garlic
- ✓ 1 teaspoon marjoram
- ✓ 1 teaspoon parsley
- ✓ 1 teaspoon onion powder
- ✓ Himalayan sea salt and pepper, to taste

1. Cut the squash in half.
2. Clean out the seeds, peel and slice to about ¼ inch thickness. You can leave them like this or chop them as I did in the photo.
3. Lay out the individual pieces on a baking sheet lined with parchment paper.
4. Coat the squash with 2 teaspoons of extra virgin olive oil. Then liberally sprinkle the herbs and spices over the squash.
5. Bake at 350° Fahrenheit until soft (about 30 minutes).
6. Makes 3 servings. 1 serving = 1 cup.

☐ Serving of protein
☐ 1 Serving of fruit

☑ 2 Servings of Vegetables
☑ 2 Servings of Healthy fat

Salads

In the past, salads have gotten a bad "rap." If you are creative with your salads, however, they can provide a bountiful abundance of beautiful colors and nutrition. Salads are not just pretty to look at but can be amazing to eat too.

"The beauty of life is in small details, not big events."

- Jim Jarmusch

Burger Salad with Mustard Dressing

- ✓ 1 cup fresh lettuce of choice chopped
- ✓ 2 ounces cooked burger
- ✓ 1/3 cup tomato sliced
- ✓ 1/3 cup onion diced
- ✓ 1 soft-boiled egg
- ✓ 1/3 cup poblano pepper, roasted
- ✓ Any other toppings of choice: jalapeños
- ✓ For the Dressing:
- ✓ 2 tablespoons mustard (NO sugar added)
- ✓ 1 tablespoon apple cider vinegar
- ✓ 2 teaspoons extra-virgin olive oil
- ✓ ¼ teaspoon freshly cracked pepper

1. Place lettuce in a large bowl.
2. Add desired toppings including your burger.
3. In a small bowl whisk together dressing ingredients.
4. Pour over salad and serve.

☑ 3 ounces of protein
☐ 1 Serving of fruit

☑ 2 Servings of Vegetables
☑ 2 Servings of Healthy fat

Strawberry Chicken Spinach Salad with Citrus Dressing

- ✓ 1/3 cup red onion slices
- ✓ 1/3 cup cucumber slices
- ✓ 1 cup strawberries chopped
- ✓ 1/3 cup roasted asparagus, chopped
- ✓ 1/8 avocado, chopped OR 6-8 almonds, toasted
- ✓ 3 ounces grilled or baked skinless chicken breast
- ✓ 1 cup of spinach

Citrus dressing:

- ✓ ½ cup fresh grapefruit juice
- ✓ Liquid Stevia, to taste
- ✓ ½ teaspoon Himalayan sea salt
- ✓ ¼ teaspoon ground pepper
- ✓ 1 teaspoon Dijon mustard (NO sugar added)
- ✓ 1 clove garlic minced
- ✓ 1 teaspoon extra virgin olive oil

1. Make dressing by whisking together all ingredients.
2. Layer salad ingredients in mason jar, if you choose. Start layering in this order: citrus dressing, onions, cucumbers, strawberries, asparagus, chicken, avocado OR almonds, and spinach.
3. When ready to serve, shake mason jar and pour into a bowl.

☑ 3 ounces of protein
☑ 1 Serving of fruit

☑ 2 Servings of Vegetables
☑ 2 Servings of Healthy fat

Grilled Veggie and Chicken Salad with Tomato Vinaigrette

For the chicken:
- ✓ 3 ounces chicken breast
- ✓ 1 teaspoon rosemary
- ✓ 1 teaspoon Italian seasoning
- ✓ ¼ teaspoon Himalayan sea salt

For the veggies:
- ✓ 1/3 cup zucchini
- ✓ 1/3 cup yellow squash
- ✓ 1/3 cup red pepper
- ✓ 1/3 cup fresh cherry tomatoes
- ✓ 1/3 cup red onion
- ✓ 1/3 cup of spinach
- ✓ 1 teaspoon extra-virgin olive oil
- ✓ 1 teaspoon Himalayan sea salt

Tomato Vinaigrette:
- ✓ ½ cup diced tomatoes, blended
- ✓ 1 tablespoon apple cider vinegar
- ✓ Dash ground black pepper
- ✓ ½ teaspoon garlic granules
- ✓ ½ teaspoon onion powder
- ✓ 1 teaspoon extra virgin olive oil
- ✓ Dash fine Himalayan sea salt
- ✓ Optional: ¼ teaspoon cayenne

1. Toss chicken in spices, set aside. Cut veggies and toss in extra virgin olive oil and Himalayan sea salt, set aside.
2. Spray the grill and heat to 350-400° Fahrenheit. Place the chicken breast on one side. On the other side place a layer of greased tin foil and place the veggies on top.
3. Cook for about 7-8 minutes then flip over. Cook veggies until desired softness and cook chicken until fully cooked.

4. Make the dressing by combining ingredients in your high-speed blender and blending until smooth. Taste and adjust spices as needed.

5. Serve with veggies warm or hot over a bed of spinach!

————————————————————

☑ 3 ounces of protein ☑ 2 Servings of Vegetables
☐ 1 Serving of fruit ☑ 1-2 Servings of Healthy fat

Blueberry Kale and Butternut Squash Salad

- ✓ ½ cup kale, washed and de-stemmed
- ✓ ¼ cup of spring mix
- ✓ 1 cup blueberries
- ✓ 6 Kalamata olives pitted and cut into slivers
- ✓ ¼ cup red or yellow bell pepper, thinly sliced
- ✓ 1 cup small butternut squash
- ✓ 1 teaspoon extra virgin olive oil (divided)
- ✓ 1 tablespoon balsamic vinegar (NO sugar added)
- ✓ ½ teaspoon Himalayan sea salt
- ✓ Freshly ground black pepper, to taste

1. Preheat oven to 400° Fahrenheit.
2. Prepare the squash by peeling it, cutting it in half and scraping out the seeds.
3. Cut the squash into 1-inch cubes, toss them in ½ teaspoon extra virgin olive oil and a pinch of Himalayan sea salt, and spread the cubes on a baking sheet.
4. Roast the squash at 400° Fahrenheit for 30-40 minutes, turning once or twice, until all the pieces are tender, and some have brown spots.
5. Remove the squash from oven when finished and let the squash cool.
6. Stack the kale leaves and roll them into tight bundles, then slice very thinly with a sharp knife to create shredded pieces.
7. In a salad bowl, whisk together dressing by combining extra virgin olive oil, balsamic vinegar, Himalayan sea salt and pepper.

Add all the remaining salad ingredients and toss everything together. Let the salad marinate in the refrigerator for at least 30 minutes to an hour before serving. The longer the kale marinates, the softer the leaves will become.

☐ Serving of protein

☑ 1 Serving of fruit

☑ 2 Servings of Vegetables

☑ 2 Servings of Healthy fat

Roasted Vegetable Salad with Shallot Vinaigrette

- ✓ ¼ cup asparagus spears, cut into 1 ½-inch pieces
- ✓ ¼ cup frozen artichoke hearts, thawed (about 2 ½ cups)
- ✓ ¼ cup Roma tomatoes, sliced ½ inch thick

- ✓ 1 teaspoon melted coconut oil
- ✓ Himalayan sea salt, to taste
- ✓ 1 cup romaine lettuce chopped
- ✓ ¼ cup roasted red bell pepper, chopped
- ✓ 1/8 ripe avocado pitted and chopped

Shallot vinaigrette:
- ✓ 2 tablespoons raw apple cider vinegar
- ✓ 1 tablespoon finely minced shallot
- ✓ 1 teaspoon extra-virgin olive oil
- ✓ 2 tablespoons water
- ✓ 2 teaspoons Dijon mustard (NO sugar added)
- ✓ 1 clove garlic minced

1. Preheat the oven to 350° Fahrenheit and line two rimmed baking sheets with parchment paper.

2. Combine the asparagus, artichoke hearts, and sliced tomatoes in a large bowl and toss with the melted coconut oil. Arrange the vegetables in a single layer on the lined baking sheets, sprinkle with Himalayan sea salt, and roast in the oven until tender, about 30 minutes. Remove from the oven and allow the vegetables to cool slightly.

3. To prepare the vinaigrette, combine the vinaigrette ingredients in a high-speed blender and blend until completely smooth. Set aside.

4. Place the chopped romaine in a large serving bowl and top with the warm roasted vegetables, roasted pepper, and chopped avocado. Pour the dressing over the top and toss well to coat. Serve immediately.

☐ Serving of protein
☑ 1 Serving of fruit

☑ 2 Servings of Vegetables
☑ 2 Servings of Healthy fat

Strawberry Avocado Arugula Salad

- ✓ 2 cups arugula, or lettuce of choice
- ✓ 1-2 tablespoons fresh lemon juiced
- ✓ 1 teaspoon extra-virgin olive oil
- ✓ 1/8 avocado, peeled, pitted, and diced
- ✓ 1 cup sliced fresh strawberries
- ✓ 1 teaspoon chopped fresh mint, plus more for garnish
- ✓ Pinch of freshly grated lemon zest, plus more to taste
- ✓ Himalayan sea salt and freshly ground black pepper, to taste

1. Toss the arugula in 1 tablespoon lemon juice and extra virgin olive oil. Gently toss the avocado with the strawberries, mint, and lemon zest. Arrange over the arugula.
2. Garnish with mint and additional lemon juice to taste. Season with Himalayan sea salt and freshly ground black pepper to taste.

☐ Serving of protein
☐ 1 Serving of fruit

☑ 2 Servings of Vegetables
☑ 2 Servings of Healthy fat

Rosemary Grilled Chicken and Peach Salad

Rosemary Grilled chicken:
- ✓ 3 ounces chicken breast
- ✓ 1 clove garlic minced
- ✓ 1 teaspoon fresh rosemary, stems removed and minced
- ✓ 1 teaspoon extra virgin olive oil

Salad:
- ✓ 1½ cups of your favorite greens, washed
- ✓ ½ cup of large red onion
- ✓ 1 ripe peach sliced
- ✓ 2 teaspoons raw apple cider vinegar
- ✓ 1 clove garlic minced
- ✓ Himalayan sea salt, to taste
- ✓ Freshly ground black pepper, to taste
- ✓ 1 teaspoon of extra-virgin olive oil
- ✓ Liquid Stevia, to taste (optional, for sweetness)

1. Combine the chicken breast with the marinade ingredients and marinate in the refrigerator for at least 1 hour, marinating overnight adds much more flavor.

2. Slice both ends off the onion and peel away the tough outer layer. Slice the onion from top to bottom into ½" thick slices. Preheat the grill over high heat until the temperature reaches 400° Fahrenheit. Place the marinated chicken and onion slices on the grill, and immediately lower the heat to medium.

3. Cook the chicken for 6-8 minutes per side, the time will depend on the thickness of your chicken. You'll know they're ready to turn over when they loosen from the grill and are easy to turn. Grill the onions for about 4 minutes per side, or until they have browned grill marks, and are starting to soften.

4. When the onions and chicken are done, remove them from the grill and set them aside to cool a bit while you finish the salad.

5. Slice the peach into ¼ " slices or cubes. Layer the peaches over the salad greens, then cut up both the chicken and onions and layer them over the salad greens.

6. Drizzle the dressing over the top or serve it with the salad. This salad is best served with the chicken and onions still a bit warm from the grill.

☑ 3 ounces of protein
☑ 1 Serving of fruit

☑ 2 Servings of Vegetables
☑ 1 Servings of Healthy fat

Red Cabbage Citrus Salad

Salad:
- ✓ 2 cups shredded cabbage
- ✓ 1 orange peeled and sliced
- ✓ 1/8 avocado diced

Dressing:
- ✓ 2 tablespoons apple cider vinegar
- ✓ 3 tablespoons lime juice (approximately one lime)
- ✓ 1 teaspoon extra virgin olive oil
- ✓ ¼ cup fresh cilantro, chopped
- ✓ ½ teaspoon chili powder
- ✓ ½ teaspoon garlic powder
- ✓ ½ teaspoon black pepper
- ✓ ½ teaspoon Himalayan sea salt

1. Shred the cabbage with a knife, grater or food processor. Put the shredded cabbage in a bowl and set aside.
2. Combine all the dressing ingredients in a jar with a lid and shake until thoroughly mixed.
3. Pour half of the dressing on the cabbage and toss until combined.
4. Top the mixture with orange slices and avocado and serve with more dressing if desired.

☐ Serving of protein
☑ 1 Serving of fruit

☑ 2 Servings of Vegetables
☑ 1-2 Servings of Healthy fat

Lime Chicken Chopped Salad

- ✓ 3 ounces chicken breast
- ✓ 1 tablespoon paprika
- ✓ 1 lime juiced
- ✓ ¼ teaspoon Himalayan sea salt
- ✓ ¼ teaspoon freshly ground pepper

Salad:
- ✓ 1 ½ cup spring mix
- ✓ 1 peach sliced
- ✓ ¼ cup grape tomatoes, sliced
- ✓ ¼ cup red onion, finely chopped
- ✓ 1/8 avocado cubed

Lime Vinaigrette:
- ✓ 1 teaspoon extra virgin olive oil
- ✓ 2 tablespoons apple cider vinegar
- ✓ 1 lime juiced
- ✓ Dash Himalayan sea salt

1. Heat the grill to medium heat.
2. Season chicken with Himalayan sea salt and pepper. In a bowl or marinade dish, combine paprika and lime.
3. Add chicken and let marinate in the fridge for at least 20 minutes; the longer the better.
4. When ready to cook, add chicken to the greased grill.
5. Cut peach into slices and add to grill for 3-4 minutes on each side.
6. While grilling, chop avocado, tomato, and red onion and add spring mix to serving dish.
7. Whisk together dressing, taste, and adjust seasoning as desired (i.e., more lime, additional Himalayan sea salt, additional vinegar) and place in fridge until ready to use.
8. When chicken is done cooking, assemble the salad, toss with dressing and enjoy!

☑ 3 ounces of protein
☑ 1 Serving of fruit

☑ 2 Servings of Vegetables
☑ 1-2 Servings of Healthy fat

Cobb Salad

✓ 1 ½ cups spring mix lettuce, tightly packed
✓ 1 hard-boiled egg sliced
✓ 1/8 avocado cut into chunks
✓ ¼ cup tomato, chopped
✓ ¼ cup red onion, chopped
✓ 2 ounces cooked, cubed chicken

Dressing:

✓ 1 teaspoon extra-virgin olive oil
✓ 1 tablespoon Bragg's apple cider vinegar
✓ Half a lemon juiced

1. If you are particular about your presentation, place the salad in a bowl and then add the toppings on in rows as the picture. If not, simply place all ingredients in a large mixing bowl, add the dressing, toss, and serve.

☑ 3 ounces of protein
☐ 1 Serving of fruit

☑ 2 Servings of Vegetables
☑ 2 Servings of Healthy fat

Steak Cobb Salad with Cilantro Vinaigrette

- ✓ 1 cup romaine lettuce
- ✓ ½ cup cherry tomatoes, diced
- ✓ 1 hard-boiled egg sliced
- ✓ ½ cup sliced red onion
- ✓ ¼ cup pickled jalapeños
- ✓ 2 ounces steak of choice sliced
- ✓ 1 teaspoon coconut oil

Cilantro-Dijon Vinaigrette:
- ✓ 1 teaspoon extra-virgin olive oil
- ✓ 2 teaspoons apple cider vinegar
- ✓ 1 teaspoon Dijon mustard (NO sugar added)
- ✓ Pinch of Himalayan sea salt
- ✓ Pinch of pepper
- ✓ ¼ cup chopped cilantro
- ✓ 1 teaspoon lemon
- ✓ Liquid Stevia, to taste

1. Preheat the oven to broil. Pat the steak dry and season generously with Himalayan sea salt and pepper.
2. Heat an oven-safe skillet with 1 teaspoon of coconut oil and let the skillet get hot. Add the steak and sear on each side for 2 minutes. Transfer to the oven and let cook for 7-11 minutes, depending on the thickness of your steak, until it reaches your desired doneness.
3. Add dressing ingredients into your high-speed blender and blend until smooth.
4. Assemble: Place lettuce, tomatoes, hard-boiled egg, red onion, and jalapeños in your salad bowls. Top with steak. Serve with dressing.

☑ 3 ounces of protein
☐ 1 Serving of fruit

☑ 2 Servings of Vegetables
☑ 2 Servings of Healthy fat

Spiced Grapefruit and Chicken Watercress Salad

3 ounces chicken breast shredded
½ pink grapefruit
1 dried red chili
1 teaspoon extra virgin olive oil
1 tablespoon lemon juice
1 tablespoon sumac
¼ cup red onion, thinly sliced
1 ½ cups watercress leaves
1/3 cup fresh basil leaves, rough chopped
¼ cup shallot
2 teaspoons apple cider vinegar
Himalayan sea salt to taste

1. Cut the ends of the grapefruit. With sharp knife, cut the rind off along with the white pith. Over a bowl to save the juice, cut the segments away from each membrane, keeping segments in another bowl. Set aside.
2. Pour the juice into a saucepan. Squeeze the other half of the grapefruit if more is needed. Add red chili, bring to a boil and reduce heat to medium and simmer. Cook until reduced.
3. Set aside to cool and then whisk in the extra-virgin olive oil, lemon juice, Himalayan sea salt to taste and the sumac.
4. Shred the chicken breast meat. Set aside.
5. Rinse and cut the watercress from the stems. Rough chop the basil and the mix all salad leaves together.
6. Gently toss the salad greens with the fruit, red onion slices, shredded chicken and the salad dressing. Save reserve dressing if needed, or for another salad. Top with shallots and serve!

☑ 3 ounces of protein
☑ 1 Serving of fruit

☑ 2 Servings of Vegetables
☑ 2 Servings of Healthy fat

Kale Ginger Detox Salad

- ✓ 1 cup kale
- ✓ 1/3 cup broccoli florets
- ✓ 1/3 cup Brussel sprouts roughly chopped
- ✓ 1/3 cup red cabbage roughly chopped
- ✓ ½ cup fresh parsley
- ✓ 6 almonds or 1 tablespoon sunflower seeds

Dressing:
- ✓ 1 teaspoon extra-virgin olive oil
- ✓ 3 tablespoons lemon juice or to taste
- ✓ 2 teaspoons fresh ginger peeled and grated
- ✓ 1 teaspoon Dijon mustard (NO sugar added) Himalayan sea salt, to taste

1. Using a food processor, process all the veggies up to the parsley until finely chopped and mix together in a large bowl. This may take a few batches.

2. Add the almonds or sunflower seeds to the food processor and pulse, until roughly chopped, and mix in with the salad.

3. In a small bowl, whisk together all the ingredients for the dressing and drizzle over top of the salad OR place in a jar and use as needed. Enjoy!

☐ Serving of protein
☐ 1 Serving of fruit

☑ 2 Servings of Vegetables
☑ 2 Servings of Healthy fat

Indoor
Holiday Celebrations

Holidays are a time for family and friends and connection to food with celebration. Feeding your body healthful foods allows you to truly connect to the festivities with more energy and life in your food and your body.

"Celebrate the happiness that friends are always giving, make every day a holiday and celebrate just living."
-Amanda Bradley

Healthy Roast Turkey

✓ 1 organic turkey
✓ ½ lb. real butter
✓ ½ teaspoon sage
✓ ½ teaspoon thyme
✓ ½ teaspoon marjoram
✓ ½ teaspoon rosemary

1. Preheat oven to 425° Fahrenheit.
2. Rinse the turkey inside and out, and then pat dry. Stuff (if desired), and truss. Cut a piece of cheesecloth to length that will cover the turkey and unfold to a single thickness.
3. Melt butter in a small saucepan and add sage, thyme, marjoram, and rosemary. Place cheesecloth in the pan and completely saturate.
4. Place turkey in oven and reduce heat to 325° Fahrenheit. After 15 minutes, drape butter-soaked cheesecloth over the turkey so that it is completely covered. After an hour, baste the turkey every 15 minutes or so to keep the cheesecloth moist. Remove the cheesecloth for the last 30 minutes of cooking time for crisp skin. After removing from oven, allow turkey to rest for at least 20 minutes before carving.
5. Serving Size = 3 ounces of turkey

☑ Serving of protein
☐ 1 Serving of fruit

☐ 2 Servings of Vegetables
☐ 2 Servings of Healthy fat

Mashed No-Tatoes

- ✓ 1 head of cauliflower
- ✓ 1 ½ tablespoons real butter
- ✓ 1-2 cloves of garlic (optional)
- ✓ Himalayan sea salt to taste
- ✓ Black pepper to taste

1. Steam cauliflower until very soft (you can also boil it, but this is not recommended as a lot of the nutrients are lost)
2. Chop up the cauliflower and put in food processor or blender with butter, salt, pepper, and garlic (if desired).
3. Blend to desired consistency.
4. Serving Size = 1 Cup

☐ Serving of protein
☐ 1 Serving of fruit

☑ 2 Servings of Vegetables
☑ 2 Servings of Healthy fat

Green Bean Cauli Casserole

- ✓ 6 cups green beans
- ✓ 2/3 cup plus 1 tablespoon olive oil, divided
- ✓ 1 package (24 oz) white mushrooms, washed and sliced
- ✓ ½ teaspoon Himalayan sea salt (to taste)
- ✓ ¼ teaspoon black pepper (to taste)
- ✓ 2 cloves garlic minced
- ✓ 1 cup shallots, cleaned, peeled, and sliced thinly
- ✓ 2 ½ cups "Mashed No-Tatoes" (see above recipe)
- ✓ ½ cup slivered almonds
- ✓ 1 tablespoon basting oil
- ✓ Grapeseed oil (for greasing)

1. Preheat oven to 350° Fahrenheit.
2. Add green beans to a stockpot of salted, boiling water; blanch 3-5 minutes, until tender. Drain; transfer to bowl of ice water. Drain; set aside
3. Heat 1 tablespoon olive oil in large skillet on Medium-High. Add mushrooms, salt, and pepper; cook, stirring 10-12 minutes until mushrooms are dry. Reduce heat to Medium-Low. Add garlic and cook, stirring 2-3 minutes. Add "Mashed No-Tatoes"; stir to combine. Cook thoroughly, stirring occasionally; season with addition- al salt and pepper to taste and stir in green beans
4. Combine slivered almonds and basting oil in a small dish; set aside
5. Grease a 9x13-inch casserole dish. Transfer green bean mixture to dish and top with slivered almond mixture. Bake 25-30 minutes
6. Makes 6 servings. 1 serving = 1 cup

☑ Serving of protein
☐ 1 Serving of fruit

☐ 2 Servings of Vegetables
☐ 2 Servings of Healthy fat

Cauliflower Pizza

- ✓ 2 cups of cauliflower
- ✓ ¼ teaspoon Himalayan sea salt
- ✓ ½ teaspoon dried basil
- ✓ ½ teaspoon dried oregano
- ✓ ½ teaspoon garlic powder
- ✓ Few shakes of crushed red pepper
- ✓ 2 tablespoons almond meal
- ✓ 1 tablespoon avocado or grapeseed oil
- ✓ 1 egg

Toppings:
- ✓ 6 ounces shredded cooked chicken
- ✓ ½ cup sautéed mushrooms
- ✓ 1/8 avocado
- ✓ ½ cup tomato sauce (NO sugar added)
- ✓ Basil

1. Place a pizza stone in the oven or baking sheet if you don't have a pizza stone. Preheat oven to 450° Fahrenheit. On a cutting board, place a large piece of parchment paper and brush the parchment with 1 teaspoon grapeseed oil.

2. Wash and thoroughly dry a small head of cauliflower. Don't get one the size of your head unless you are planning on making 2 pizzas. Cut off the florets; you don't need many stems; just the florets. Pulse in your food processor for about 30 seconds, until you get

powdery snow-like cauliflower. Measure out 2 cups of cauliflower. Place the cauliflower in a microwave-safe bowl and cover. Microwave for 4 minutes. Dump cooked cauliflower onto a clean tea towel and allow to cool for a bit before
attempting the next step. When cauliflower is cool enough to handle, wrap it up in the dish towel and wring out the water. You want to squeeze out as much water as possible. This will ensure you get a chewy pizza-like crust instead of a crumbly mess.

3. Dump cauliflower into a bowl. Now add all your spices, your almond meal, and the extra virgin olive oil. Mix the mixture to incorporate all the ingredients. Now add your egg and mix away again. Hands tend to work best. When mixed, use your hands to form the dough into a crust on your oiled parchment paper. Pat it down thoroughly; you want it nice and tightly formed together. Don't make it too thick or thin.

4. Using a cutting board, slide the parchment paper onto your hot pizza stone or baking sheet in the oven. Bake for about 12 minutes, or until it starts to turn golden brown and the edges crisp up. Remove from oven. Go off looks rather than time; you want the edges to start to be crispy brown but not too much so when you cook
it again after adding toppings it will burn. Add your toppings and slide parchment with topped pizza back in the hot oven and cook for another 5 minutes until the toppings are warm. Enjoy!

5. Makes 2 Servings. 1 serving = half the cauliflower pizza.

☑ 3 ounces of protein   ☑ 2 Servings of Vegetables
☐ 1 Serving of fruit   ☑ 2 Servings of Healthy fat

Healthful Chili

- ✓ 1½ pounds ground beef
- ✓ 2 cloves garlic chopped
- ✓ 2 tablespoons extra virgin olive oil
- ✓ 1½ cups onion, diced, about 1 large onion
- ✓ ½ cup chopped celery, about 1 stalk
- ✓ 2 tablespoons chili powder
- ✓ 1 teaspoon ground cumin
- ✓ 1 teaspoon oregano
- ✓ 1 teaspoon Himalayan sea salt
- ✓ ¼ teaspoon cayenne pepper
- ✓ 4 cups zucchini, diced, about 2-3 medium zucchini
- ✓ One 15-ounce can tomato sauce
- ✓ One 15-ounce can dice tomatoes

1. In your seasoned or 5-6-quart large cast iron pot, brown beef and garlic. Cook over medium heat until beef is thoroughly cooked and browned. Drain off excess fat, set aside.

2. Add extra virgin olive oil, onions, celery, and seasonings to the skillet and cook until translucent over medium-high heat, about 5-7 minutes. When onions are golden, and veggies are midway cooked, add zucchini and cook for 2 minutes, making sure you stir everything well.

3. Add cooked beef, tomato sauce, and tomatoes into the pot and stir well. Bring everything to a boil, stirring frequently, reduce heat and simmer for 20 minutes.

4. Check on the mixture every so often and stir. Serve immediately.

5. Makes 8 servings. 1 serving = 1 3/4 cup.

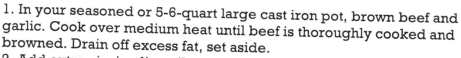

☑ 3 ounces of protein
☐ 1 Serving of fruit

☑ 2 Servings of Vegetables
☑ 2 Servings of Healthy fat

Delicious Broccoli and Cauliflower Rice

- ✓ 1 cup Cauliflower
- ✓ 1 cup Broccoli
- ✓ 2 teaspoons extra virgin olive oil
- ✓ 1 teaspoon garlic powder
- ✓ Himalayan sea salt + Pepper to taste

1. Preheat oven to 350° Fahrenheit.
2. Cut the cauliflower and broccoli into small florets. Process them in a food processor until they are fine and resemble rice.
3. Dump the mixture on a large cookie sheet. Season with Himalayan sea salt, pepper and the extra virgin olive oil. Mix and spread the cauliflower and broccoli on the sheet.
4. Bake for 10 minutes. Remove from oven and stir. Spread the mixture again and allow to bake for another 10 minutes. Repeat the above process until it begins to golden.
5. Makes 1 serving. Enjoy!

☐ Serving of protein
☐ 1 Serving of fruit

☑ 2 Servings of Vegetables
☑ 2 Servings of Healthy fat

Mock Sweet Potato Casserole

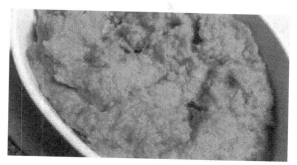

- ✓ 4 cups cauliflower
- ✓ 1 cup mashed pumpkin
- ✓ ¾ teaspoon liquid stevia
- ✓ 3 eggs
- ✓ ½ teaspoon Himalayan sea salt
- ✓ 3 tablespoons real butter softened
- ✓ 1 teaspoon cinnamon
- ✓ 1 teaspoon nutmeg
- ✓ ½ teaspoon ginger

1. Cut cauliflower into florets and steam until soft
2. Combine steamed cauliflower, pumpkin, and ginger in food processor or blender. Puree until smooth.
3. Spread mashed cauliflower mixture into a 2 quart or 11x17 casserole dish.
4. Bake at 325° Fahrenheit for 30 minutes.
5. Makes 6 servings. 1 serving = ½ cup

☑ 1.5 ounces of protein
☑ 1 Serving of fruit

☑ 1 Servings of Vegetables
☑ 3 Servings of Healthy fat

Baked Apple

✓ 1-2 teaspoons real butter divided
✓ 1 green apple
✓ ¼ teaspoon cinnamon

1. Preheat the oven to 350° Fahrenheit. Melt 1 teaspoon of butter: I place it in the cast iron dish and gently warm it on the stovetop until the butter is liquid, then turn the heat off and set the dish aside until ready to use.
2. Halve, core, and thinly slice the apple. You want the slices to be about 1/16-inch thick. More than 1/8-inch and they will take a long time to soften.
3. Start layering the apple slices into the dish, slightly overlapping them. I do the outside circumference of the dish first, then did another circle inside that.
4. Sprinkle the cinnamon on top of the apples and dot the extra teaspoon of butter over the top of the apples if you want; this is optional.
5. Bake for about 20 minutes or until the apple has softened and begun to brown slightly at the edges. Serve warm.

___

☐ Serving of protein
☑ 1 Serving of fruit

☐ 2 Servings of Vegetables
☑ 1-2 Servings of Healthy fat

Cranberry Sauce

- ✓ 1-12 oz. bag of fresh or frozen cranberries
- ✓ 1 cup Xylitol
- ✓ 1 cup water
- ✓ ½ teaspoon cinnamon
- ✓ Grated orange zest to taste

1. Bring water and Xylitol to a boil in a medium saucepan
2. Add cranberries to water and return to a boil
3. Add cinnamon and orange zest
4. Reduce heat and boil gently for 10 minutes, stirring occasionally
5. Pour sauce into bowl; cover and cool completely at room temperature or refrigerate until serving time *the longer you cook, the thicker it will be.
6. Serving size = ½ cup

☐ Serving of protein
☐ 1/2 Serving of fruit

☐ 2 Servings of Vegetables
☑ 1-2 Servings of Healthy fat

Outdoor

Holiday Celebrations

Barbeques and other outdoor celebrations are a time to kick back, relax, and enjoy the beauty of nature. You can still feed your body healthfully with these amazing recipes and enjoy all that the outdoor seasons offer in celebration!

"The more you praise and celebrate your life, the more there is in life to be celebrated"

-Oprah Winfrey

Sweet and Crunchy Chicken Slaw

- ✓ 1 cup red cabbage
- ✓ 2/3 cups white cabbage
- ✓ 1/3 cup scallions chopped
- ✓ 3 ounces organic chicken shredded
- ✓ 6 slivered almonds
- ✓ 1 teaspoon Grass fed butter
- ✓ 1 tablespoon pumpkin seeds
- ✓ 1 tablespoon apple cider vinegar
- ✓ 1 teaspoon extra-virgin olive oil
- ✓ 1 tablespoon Bragg's liquid aminos
- ✓ Optional: Liquid Stevia for sweetness

1. In a bowl, mix shredded red cabbage, white cabbage, and shredded chicken (prepare chicken beforehand; either by poaching it, or using shredded crockpot chicken).
2. In a small bowl, whisk together apple cider vinegar, extra virgin olive oil, Bragg's liquid aminos, and Stevia.
3. Add the dressing to the cabbage and chicken and mix well.
4. In a pan, heat 1 teaspoon butter and sauté almonds and pumpkin seeds for 2-4 minutes.
5. Remove and add to the bowl.
6. Chop scallions and add into the bowl. Mix well and serve.

☑ 3 ounces of protein   ☑ 2 Servings of Vegetables
☐ 1 Serving of fruit   ☑ 2 Servings of Healthy fat

Easy Veggie Salad

- ✓ ½ cup organic cucumbers, finely chopped
- ✓ ½ cup organic ripe tomatoes, finely chopped
- ✓ ¼ cup red onion, finely chopped
- ✓ ¼ cup green pepper, finely chopped
- ✓ ½ cup cauliflower, grated into cauliflower 'rice'
- ✓ 1/3 cup fresh Italian parsley finely chopped
- ✓ 1-2 teaspoons extra-virgin olive oil
- ✓ 1 tablespoon lemon juice, more to taste
- ✓ Himalayan sea salt and freshly ground pepper, to taste
- ✓ Optional: ground garlic, to taste
- ✓ Optional: 1/3 cup scallions, finely chopped

1.Finely chop cucumbers, tomatoes, and onions and combine in a large mixing bowl.
2. In a food processor, pulse parsley until fine (or chop by hand)
3. Combine chopped parsley into bowl and mix well.
4. Pour lemon juice and extra-virgin olive oil over vegetables and mix well to coat. Add scallions, ground garlic, Himalayan sea salt, and freshly ground pepper to taste. Taste and adjust seasoning as desired.
5. Cover and refrigerate until ready to serve.
Tip: to prevent salad from getting too watery, scoop out seeds of the tomatoes before chopping.
6. In a food processor (or by hand using a grater), pulse/grate cauliflower until it's a fine-rice consistency. Add cauliflower rice into salad bowl and mix well to combine. Cover and refrigerate until ready to serve.

☐ Serving of protein
☐ 1 Serving of fruit

☑ 2 Servings of Vegetables
☑ 2 Servings of Healthy fat

Baked Cinnamon Apple Chips

✓ 1 Granny Smith apple
✓ 1 teaspoon cinnamon

1. Preheat oven to 200° Fahrenheit.
2. Using a sharp knife, slice apple thinly. Discard seeds. Prepare a baking sheet with parchment paper and arrange apple slices without overlapping. Sprinkle cinnamon over apples.
3. Bake for approximately 1 hour, then flip. Continue baking for 1-2 hours, flipping occasionally, until the apple slices are no longer moist. Store in airtight container.

☐ Serving of protein
☑ 1 Serving of fruit

☐ 2 Servings of Vegetables
☐ 1-2 Servings of Healthy fat

Chicken Wings

- ✓ 2 pounds organic chicken wings

Dry Rub:
- ✓ 1 tablespoon granulated garlic
- ✓ 1 tablespoon cayenne pepper
- ✓ 1 tablespoon dry mustard
- ✓ 1 tablespoon freshly cracked black pepper
- ✓ 2 teaspoons ground cumin

Sauce:
- ✓ 2 tablespoons extra-virgin olive oil
- ✓ 4 tablespoon organic butter
- ✓ 2 tablespoon reserved dry rub
- ✓ 1 (12-ounce) bottle Frank's hot sauce
- ✓ 1 tablespoon apple cider vinegar

1.Combine all dry rub spices in a large bowl. Reserve 2 tablespoons of the mixture.

2. Add the wings to bowl and mix thoroughly. Cover and refrigerate for at least an hour.

3. Preheat oven to 375° Fahrenheit.

4. Line a baking sheet with parchment paper. Lay all wings flat on the baking sheet and bake for an hour turning halfway through.

5. When the wings are almost done, melt the butter and then add other sauce ingredients.

6. When ready to serve, add the wings to a large serving bowl, pour sauce over the wings and toss. Or throw it all in a large zip-top bag and shake!

7. Each wing has approximately ½ ounce of protein. 6 wings equal.

☑ 3 ounces of protein
☐ 1 Serving of fruit

☐ 2 Servings of Vegetables
☑ 2 Servings of Healthy fat

Turkey Sliders and Avocado Slaw

For the Burgers:
- ✓ 1lb ground turkey
- ✓ ¼ red onion, minced
- ✓ ¼ red onion, thinly sliced
- ✓ ½ poblano pepper, diced
- ✓ ½ red bell pepper, diced
- ✓ 1 teaspoon ground cumin
- ✓ ½ teaspoon ground red pepper
- ✓ Himalayan sea salt and pepper, to taste
- ✓ 1 tablespoon extra-virgin olive oil

For the Slaw:
- ✓ 1 small head of cabbage or bag of cabbage chopped
- ✓ 2 avocados
- ✓ 1 tablespoon extra-virgin olive oil
- ✓ 1 teaspoon lime juice
- ✓ ½ teaspoon lemon juice
- ✓ 1 teaspoon ground cumin
- ✓ ½ teaspoon crushed red pepper
- ✓ Himalayan sea salt and pepper, to taste

1. First, make your burgers. Add all your ingredients for your burger
in a large bowl. Shape small burger patties.
2. Heat up a large skillet over medium heat with a bit of oil and add
your sliders. Flip after about 3-5 minutes or when you see the sides
of your sliders begin to turn a white color.
3. Now make your slaw. Pull out your handy dandy food processor,
add all your ingredients for the slaw other than the cabbage and
pulse until smooth.

4. Pour your avocado "mayo" on the cabbage and mix. Top off with a bit of Himalayan sea salt and pepper.
5. Place your cabbage on a plate and top off with your sliders!
6. Makes 5 servings. 1 Serving = 3 ounces turkey burger and 2 teaspoons avocado slaw.

☑ 3 ounces of protein   ☐ 2 Servings of Vegetables
☐ 1 Serving of fruit   ☑ 2 Servings of Healthy fat

Spaghetti and Meatball Bites

- ✓ 1 medium spaghetti squash cut in half lengthwise, seeds removed
- ✓ 1lb Grass fed Ground Beef
- ✓ 1 (14oz) can tomato sauce
- ✓ 3 egg whites whisked
- ✓ 1 tablespoon dried parsley
- ✓ 1 tablespoon dried basil
- ✓ 1 tablespoon dried thyme
- ✓ Himalayan sea salt and pepper, to taste
- ✓ 1 tablespoon extra-virgin olive oil

1. Preheat oven to 425° Fahrenheit. Cut spaghetti squash in half lengthwise, use a spoon to remove the seeds and excess threads.
2. Place spaghetti squash cut side down on a baking sheet and bake for 20-25 minutes. Make sure not to overcook!
3. Add your ground beef to a large bowl and add ½ tablespoon of parsley, basil, and thyme and a bit of Himalayan sea salt and pepper. Combine.
4. Make your ground beef into small bite-sized meatballs. In a large skillet over medium heat, add your extra virgin olive oil, then small meatballs. Add your jar of tomato sauce, extra herbs, and Himalayan sea salt and pepper.
5. After meatballs have cooked for about 3-4 minutes, flip them and let them simmer in the sauce.
6. While the meatballs are cooking through, remove your spaghetti squash from oven and use a fork to de-thread the squash. Turn oven down to 350° Fahrenheit. Place silicone cups in your muffin tin and

add your spaghetti squash threads to each silicone cup, pressing down in the middle of the cup for the meatball to sit.

7. When the meatballs are done cooking, remove them from the sauce and place each in a muffin tin. Now pour just a little bit of beaten egg white on top of each muffin, spaghetti squash, and the meatball.

8. Bake for 18-20 minutes or until egg is completely cooked through.

9. Serving Size = One 3-ounce meatball with 2 cups of spaghetti squash

---

☑ 3 ounces of protein
☐ 1 Serving of fruit

☑ 2 Servings of Vegetables
☑ 1 Servings of Healthy fat

Jalapeno Deviled Eggs

✓ 6 eggs
✓ ¼ cup Vegenaise
✓ 1 tablespoon minced jalapeño (leave some pieces behind for garnishing)
✓ 1/8 teaspoon smoked paprika
✓ ¼ teaspoon Himalayan sea salt

1. Bring a large pot of water to boil. When the water is boiling, place eggs in the water and cook for 15 minutes. Remove from water and place in a bowl of cold water to help cool.
2. After eggs have cooled, cut eggs in half. Scoop out the yolks, place yolks in a bowl and smash with a fork. Add Vegenaise and mix well until mixture is smooth.
3. Add jalapeño and smoked paprika and Himalayan sea salt and mix well.
4. Place the yolk mixture into a small zip-top plastic bag, cut off the end and squeeze mixture into egg white halves. Garnish with left over jalapeño. Chill before serving.
5. Serving Size = 2 eggs or 4 egg halves

☑ 3 ounces of protein
☐ 1 Serving of fruit

☐ 2 Servings of Vegetables
☑ 2 Servings of Healthy fat

Salmon Dip

- ✓ One 3-ounce fillet of wild caught salmon - approx. 4 oz. before baking
- ✓ Pinch of Himalayan sea salt
- ✓ Grapeseed oil spray - for prepping dish
- ✓ Balsamic Vinegar
- ✓ 1 tablespoon extra-virgin olive oil or grapeseed oil
- ✓ Mrs. Dash (of your choice) - I use the yellow lid - Original or the Green Lid - Table Variety. But any will work.
- ✓ 1 tablespoon Vegenaise or grapeseed oil

1. If using frozen fillet, heat oven to 425° Fahrenheit. If using thawed, then heat oven to 350° Fahrenheit.

2. Using grapeseed oil, spray 9 x 11" dish to keep fish from sticking and to aid in cleaning. Place fillet in dish. Pour balsamic oil liberally over fillet. Pour 1 tablespoon of grapeseed oil over fish.

3. Liberally season with Mrs. Dash (of your choice) and small amount of Himalayan sea salt. Bake for 30 minutes until fish flakes easily.

4. Let cool for approx. 5 to 10 minutes. Place fish in a bowl and flake with a fork.

5. Add 1 tablespoon Vegenaise and mix until dip-like. You can eat with celery or serve with other veggies.

☑ 3 ounces of protein
☐ 1 Serving of fruit

☐ 2 Servings of Vegetables
☑ 1-2 Servings of Healthy fat

Low Carb Cauliflower Hummus

✓ 4 cups cauliflower florets (loosely measured, not packed in tight)
✓ 2 tablespoons water
✓ 2 tablespoons extra virgin olive oil
✓ ½ teaspoon Himalayan sea salt
✓ 1-½ teaspoons minced garlic
✓ 1-½ tablespoons tahini paste
✓ 3 tablespoons lemon juice
✓ 1 teaspoon minced garlic (in addition to above)
✓ 3 tablespoons extra virgin olive oil (in addition to above)
✓ ½ teaspoon Himalayan sea salt (in addition to above)
✓ Paprika (garnish, optional)

1. Combine the cauliflower, water, 2 tablespoons extra virgin olive oil, ½ teaspoon Himalayan sea salt and 1 ½ teaspoon minced garlic in a microwave-safe dish. Microwave uncovered for about 15 minutes - or until softened and darkened in color.

2. Put the cauliflower mixture into a blender or food processor. Add the tahini paste, lemon juice, 1 teaspoon minced garlic, 3 tablespoons extra virgin olive oil and ¼ teaspoon Himalayan sea salt. Blend until smooth. Taste and adjust seasoning as necessary.

3. To serve, place the hummus in a bowl and drizzle with extra olive oil and a sprinkle of paprika. Use red, green, and yellow sweet peppers, cucumbers, cherry tomatoes, and celery to dip with.

4. Makes 2 servings. 1 serving = 1 cup

☐ Serving of protein
☐ 1 Serving of fruit
☑ 2 Servings of Vegetables
☑ 2 Servings of Healthy fat

Mock Tail's

Mock-Tail's

Poolside Bubble

✓ 12 ounces chilled seltzer water
✓ ½ orange sliced
✓ ½ lime sliced
✓ 2 drops liquid Stevia

1. Put all ingredients in chilled glass and serve immediately

Mock-Tail's

Fruity Hibiscus Refresher

- ✓ 8 ounces Herbal Hibiscus Tea, chilled
- ✓ ½ orange sliced and squeezed
- ✓ 4 drops liquid Stevia
- ✓ 1 lemon slice
- ✓ 1 lime slice

1. Put all ingredients in tall wine glass with ice and enjoy!

Mock-Tail's

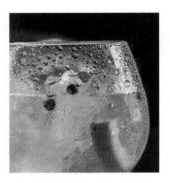

Orange Ginger Spritzer

- ✓ 8 ounces Seltzer
- ✓ 1 tsp. grated ginger
- ✓ ½ orange, juiced
- ✓ 4 drops liquid Stevia

1. Combine all ingredients in a beautiful chilled glass and serve with a slice of orange.

Mock-Tail's

Orange-Lemonade Mock Tail

- ✓ 8 ounces plain chilled seltzer water
- ✓ Juice of ½ lemon
- ✓ Juice of ½ orange
- ✓ 5 drops liquid Stevia

1. Mix all ingredients together in a glass and enjoy!

Mock-Tail's

Lime Turmeric Tonic

- ✓ 8 ounces chilled seltzer water
- ✓ ¼ tsp. turmeric
- ✓ Juice of ½ lime
- ✓ 4 drops liquid Stevia

1. Combine all ingredients together in a tall glass, serve with a slice of lime and enjoy!

Desserts

Desserts can be a delicious and nutritious way to end a meal. These healthful recipes are a great way to create the beginning of a beautiful, energized evening.

"Work is the meat of life, pleasure the dessert."

- B.C. Forbes

Grilled Peaches

✓ 1 ripe peach
✓ ¼ cup chopped almonds
✓ 1-2 teaspoons cinnamon
✓ 1 teaspoon melted coconut oil
✓ Optional: Liquid Stevia, to taste

1. Slice the peach in half and place face up on plate. Drizzle with coconut oil and season generously with cinnamon.
2. Transfer face-down to hot grill and let cook for 8-12 minutes.
3. Remove and top with liquid Stevia as desired and almonds. Enjoy!

☐ Serving of protein
☑ 1 Serving of fruit

☐ 2 Servings of Vegetables
☑ 2 Servings of Healthy fat

Adam s Apple Sauce

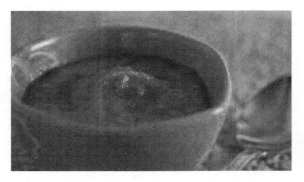

✓ 3lb bag green apples, cored and sliced
✓ 12 ounces frozen raspberries or strawberries
✓ 1 teaspoon cinnamon
✓ 1/3 cup water

1. Combine ingredients in crockpot and cook on low for 4 ½ hours
2. Mash using a potato masher
3. Leave the lid off the crockpot for the last 30 minutes of cook time to allow it to thicken
4. 1 serving = 4ounces

_____

☐ Serving of protein   ☐ 2 Servings of Vegetables
☑ 1 Serving of fruit   ☐ 2 Servings of Healthy fat

Sweet Blackberry Compote

✓ 1 cup blackberries, frozen
✓ 1/8 cup water
✓ 10 drops liquid Stevia
✓ 1 teaspoon pure vanilla extract

1. Put all ingredients into saucepan.
2. Let lightly simmer for 10 minutes until fruit has softened and broken open.
3. Serve alone or on top of pancakes (recipe in breakfast section).

☐ Serving of protein   ☐ 2 Servings of Vegetables
☑ 1 Serving of fruit   ☐ 2 Servings of Healthy fat

Pumpkin "Pie"

Crust:
- ✓ ¼ cup finely ground almonds
- ✓ 1 teaspoon grapeseed oil
- ✓ Grapeseed oil for greasing

Filling:
- ✓ 1 (15 oz.) can pumpkin puree

Crust:
- ✓ 2 teaspoons pumpkin pie spice
- ✓ ¾ cup organic pure powdered stevia for baking
- ✓ 3 eggs
- ✓ 1 cup unsweetened almond milk

1. Lightly grease an 8x8-inch baking pan with grapeseed oil
2. Distribute ground almonds evenly on the bottom and slightly up the sides of the baking pan

Filling:
1. Whisk together the puree, pumpkin pie spice, and stevia adjusting spices and stevia to taste
2. Whisk in the eggs and almond milk
3. Pour over almonds in baking dish
4. Bake at 350° Fahrenheit for 45-50 minutes (or until knife inserted in center comes out clean).
5. Chill and serve
6. Makes 6 servings

☑ 1 ounce of protein   ☑ 1 Servings of Vegetables
☐ 1 Serving of fruit   ☑ 2 Servings of Healthy fat

Charlie's Apple Crumble

Filling:
- ✓ 9 Granny Smith Apples peeled and chopped
- ✓ Juice of 1 whole lemon
- ✓ Zest of 1 lemon
- ✓ ½ cup water
- ✓ 40 drops liquid Stevia
- ✓ 1 ½ tsp cinnamon
- ✓ Pinch of ginger
- ✓ Pinch of allspice
- ✓ Pinch of nutmeg

For the topping:
- ✓ 1 cup almond flour OR ¾ cup of almond flour and ¼ almond slivers
- ✓ 1 tablespoon butter

1. Preheat oven to 350° Fahrenheit.
2. Put apples, lemon juice, lemon zest, water, Stevia, cinnamon, ginger, and allspice into saucepan and heat on medium for 5-7 minutes, stirring frequently. Heat until apples soften slightly.
3. Next, combine almond flour and 1 tbsp. melted butter in bowl and mix.
4. In 8 x 8 baking dish place apple mixture from step 2.
5. Sprinkle almond flour and butter mixture over top of apples and sprinkle slivered almonds sparingly over top.
6. Bake in oven at 350° Fahrenheit for 20 minutes. Let cool briefly and enjoy!
7. Makes 9 Servings

☐ Serving of protein
☑ 1 Serving of fruit

☐ 2 Servings of Vegetables
☑ 1 Servings of Healthy fat

Kaiya's Balsamic Peach Compote

- ✓ 1 Cup diced peaches, Frozen or Fresh
- ✓ 1 Tsp. Balsamic Vinegar
- ✓ 1/8 Cup water

1. Place peaches, water, and liquid Stevia into saucepan.
2. Let simmer for 10 minutes until peaches have softened and broken open.
3. Add Balsamic Vinegar and let simmer for 5 more minutes.
4. Cool slightly and serve.

☐ Serving of protein
☑ 1 Serving of fruit

☐ 2 Servings of Vegetables
☐ 1 Servings of Healthy fat

About the Authors

Dr. Jamie Leighow, D.C.
&
JoAnise Leighow

With a passion to help others lead a healthy lifestyle, the Leighows began developing a weight loss and nutrition program. In June 2013 they launched weight loss services as a niche within Twin Hills Chiropractic Health Center. The goal of their program is to help people lose weight and keep it off with a natural sustainable weight loss program. To date, their program has helped thousands lose weight, change their physiological health and lead healthier and happier lives.

Jamie & JoAnise believe a lifestyle focused around "Healthy Eats" extends the quantity and quality of one's life, and they strive to live out these same ideals in their personal lives. The Leighows live on a farm in Unityville, PA where they own Hereford beef cattle. They have a daughter, Jayden, and a son, Justus.

Wendi Francis MS, RD, CPC

Wendi Francis MS, RD, CPC is a pioneer in her field with specialty areas in food psychology and eating issues.

She is a graduate level registered dietitian with extensive certifications in multiple areas of psychology and nutrition.

Wendi has worked in her own private practice and business for the past twenty-five plus years facilitating permanent transformation for others by turning their fears around food into freedom.

She is a best-selling author, facilitative entrepreneur, podcast personality, recognized speaker and educator.

In this recipe book Wendi brings the inspiration to make creative cooking changes to your food enabling you to live the healthful life you were designed to live.

Made in the USA
Middletown, DE
18 January 2020

83184749R00106